LEAN HARDWARE STARTUP

How to Win the Game of Advancing Complexity

by disRaptors

www.disraptors.tech

featuring

AbilityMatrix

www.abilitymatrix.com

2020-2021

Years many of us wish to have never happened

Disclaimer 1

This book may seem to be part of the LEAN Series, started by Eric Reies' Lean Startup.
It could be, but it is not. They have great books, e.g. Lean customer development by Cindy Alvarez. All of them are highly recommended to read.

Disclaimer 2

We wrote this book with the current knowledge and experience we had. Every day new aspects and risks can appear, which may form this ecosystem. Location, tech booms, people topics, global politics, etc.

We will try to keep this book up to date in any form to give you valid support in the future.

Disclaimer 3

In the book I, We and You are used. 'I' stands for the author, András, 'We' is used for both András, and Ákos as the featured author, and 'You' means the reader, as present or future hardware startup founder.

LEAN HARDWARE STARTUP

Copyright © 2021 by disRaptors
Written by András and Krisztina Bence-Kiss
Published by András Bence-Kiss
First edition: March 2022

ISBN 978-615-01-4043-8 (print)
ISBN 978-615-01-4044-5 (epub)
ISBN 978-615-01-4045-2 (mobi)

◁ Booxpert
Publishing manager: Bence Borsos (booxpert.hu)
Cover design by György Lénárd
Interior design by György Madarász
Proofreading by Krisztina Bence-Kiss

Content

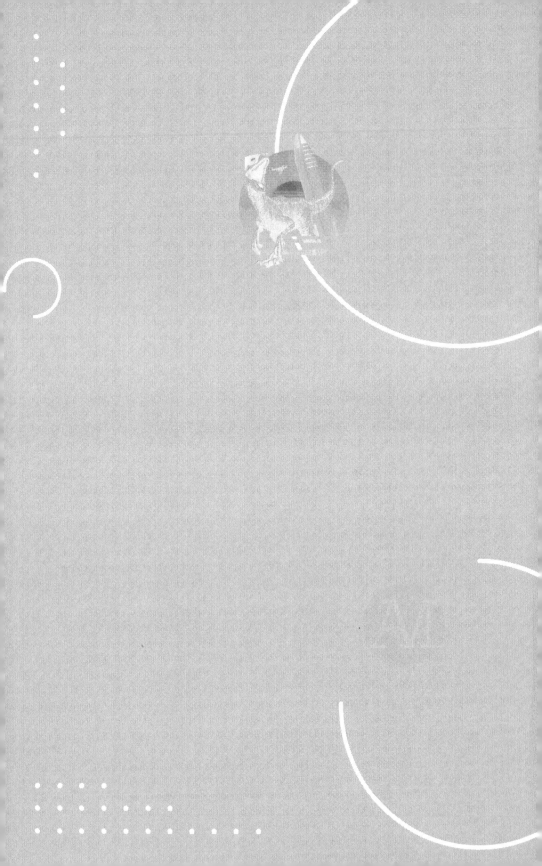

#0 Hardware is hard

Is hardware really that hard?

Yes. Manageable hard,
and easier than ever*

We will help you on your journey

---

* If the global semiconductor (or other critical) supply chain is not crashed
  at the moment.

#1 Omelet or Spacewalk?

"Hardware is hard. It's called hardware for a reason."
Marc Andreessen

Lean startup, Agile, 3D printing, FPGA (field-programmable gate array), Raspberry PI – just a few of the methods and tools that supposedly make the life of hardware startups as easy as software startups. If you are a first-time founder, getting an explanation of all the complexity of how to do hardware startup right is probably mission impossible. Marc Andreessen, a renowned investor, is famous for this phrase for a reason.

Most hardware startup founders come from the software scene, with more or less success and experience gained there. Starting a hardware startup could be less influenced by business people, since at the core of the innovation you find only tech problems – or this is what many hardware startup founders think in most cases. It takes only the first try with a hardware startup to understand how different it is from any software startup you encountered before.

To start with the obvious, it has a hardware layer. It looks like an additional layer to the technical complexity, but it also adds a lot to the business complexity of the project and a (sometimes literally speaking) cargo ship's load of problems to the development process. There is also a good reason for investors to back off from investing in hardware startups. We will analyze them one by one!

In general, investors will be looking for the best manufacturing in terms of quality and costs.

In ideal cases, most hardware stuff can be made out of off-the-shelf parts and products. If not, manufacturing costs could be a nightmare. If you want to manufacture, it can cost millions, if you outsource it and it is something special, the one-time cost may also be high. The easiest way is to buy a lot of already-existing building blocks cheaply. But where should one store it then? This is probably one of the most important differences between hardware and software influencing the price, which is called BOM (bill of material) cost.

Often, investors suggest startups outsource production to the Far East for financial reasons. Chinese manufacturing can be cheap, practically with investment costs close to zero. On the other hand, protecting assets, e.g. intellectual property is much harder there. If they can copy it, they will; and they will also improve it, and in a heartbeat, there will be a new factory next door producing a better product than yours. The biggest challenge is how to protect your IP, even if you are just outsourcing the production of parts or subassemblies. China has changed a lot, but in a country where a whole factory is built and all the assets and workers redirected overnight to a new parallel facility, you cannot be safe.

Add to that the logistical nightmare we have been living in since late 2019. The kg or volume-specific costs are 5-10x higher than in previous years and the transportation times cannot be met even if you book an air freight express delivery.

At the same time, you need to acquire customers, do marketing and sales, just like any other (software) startup, which is not a cost-free action either. In this case, scaling is what matters. You cannot copy the well-developed Saas startup methods. You cannot start with 2-10 homegrown customers. You cannot start small. After you know what to do, you need to scale right into an SME size with all the engineering departments, mechanical, electrical, investments, and of course software. Regardless of your manufacturing model, you will have investment costs, quality issues and questions, a supply chain to be kept alive, a logistic chain to be set up, a product lifecycle to be maintained, and general product compliance. Whether you hunt down experts or start with juniors, the road will be bumpy. This is the cost of the speed and knowledge game, which we will get to later in chapters #7 and #8.

Just like a software startup, you have to develop software as well, as a crucial part of the solution. The self-induced poison is the onboard or embedded software component when you code the hardware with a clear purpose to work according to your expectations – at least in theory. Thanks to the progress of the past 30 years, it has become extremely affordable, but it is still a special skill set you will need. It is not your 6-week-long coding school that will make you develop the FPGA or a complete driver that controls the functionality of your product – if you even know what that is at the beginning of your project. So, instead of your single (or double: back-end + front-end) software, now you have one more layer: embedded, back-end, front-end, where the core of the product is the synergy of these 3.

The next critical point is product compliance in depth. Depending on the field you operate in, the authorities will give you a hard time with all the certificates and permissions required to launch your product on the market, e.g. UN, IEC, CE, FDA, etc. You cannot play the Uber game saying 'the regulations are bad, so we don't give a damn about them, and are going to sell it without the certifications anyway'. If, at any point, a customs officer opens the bag for inspection and you don't have the proper approvals, or the documents are not compliant with the local regulations, you are done. Not to mention, if somebody is injured or, in the worst case, dies due to a design issue of a product lacking legal compliance (which changes from country to country), it is not a small everyday business problem, it is something you can go to jail for.

One of the most neglected business processes is pricing, or, to be exact, the awareness of what the price should cover. Founders have little or no idea of the distribution channels, Incoterms, shipping costs, complications, supply chain construction, local service desk provision, or the price you pay to have a reseller or distributor. Even if you target the right customer segment, innovators and early adopters will not pay the high price required to maintain a whole value chain and distribution channel in all cases. Relying too much on those, who are the most receptive to innovation is a common business model issue.

As you can see, the key decisions in timing, resources, and business model are similar to other types of startups, but with some extra seasoning: the complexity of the hardware layer, which makes you spend more time over the planning desk.

To highlight the difference in one analogy, think about building software startups as mastering the art of making an omelet. A broad variety of recipes are available and they are all validated to work. Preparation is relatively cheap and fast, so you just need to choose a recipe, consider the one fitting your empty stomach the best and there you are: you are almost a cook. If your first, second, or third omelets are still not perfect, you can try as many times as you want, it will be relatively cheap. Success is waiting for you. Short preparation, low cost, fast delivery, rapid repeatability – these all make it manageable for you.

On the other hand, building a hardware startup is like a spacewalk. You decide on the career path, start studying, study for long years and prove your abilities in many different ways. After 20 years, there you are, right before launch, which had been prepared for at least 5 years. You arrive at the space station and prepare for your 7-minute spacewalk for another 3-5 weeks. It is a one-time opportunity, where the opportunity window is very limited. Time, location, position, equipment, backup system, emergency plan, next opportunity window, and many other factors HAVE TO BE there without any of them missing, to even start your first step.

#2 About this book

When we started to write this book in 2020, for the majority of people who even knew the term, a startup meant a software solution, an app, a SaaS, or some other kind of digital stuff. Everybody wanted to be a startupper and change the world. On the other hand, there were hardly any hardware startups that could be called successful. There were some, who made services based on a physical product, but rarely a classical tangible product with product development, prototyping, production, distribution, and spare parts.

The whole ecosystem has been built around young people, about to do something, e.g. changing the world, bringing disruption, solving issues the last decades could not. Innovation through rapid growth, endless free work hours, and some pizza-coke combo, this is what they are destined for. With less and less domain knowledge necessary, low code startups are the newest hype, where the only hardware involved are smartphones, laptops, Macs, or PCs.

Everything started with young graduates, fully charged, motivated, bright-minded. The big universities had great courses and great lecturers with valid knowledge and a challenging attitude nurturing the first startup generations to become more entrepreneurial. Small businesses have always been an important part of the economy and not everybody tends to be an employee. The great era started with these small ventures – now known as the tech giants of Silicon Valley.

This startup mindset slowly expanded to active university students and nowadays there are idea/innovation competitions and hackathons even for children in primary schools. You cannot start hustling early enough, right?

Many founders fall into the feeling of invulnerability, power, and motivation just because of calling themselves a startupper or a CEO, but just like in the case of falling in love, one tends to see everything less objectively, so the rewards, as the risks. This type of blindness can make the ride on the rollercoaster more fun when it is up and much worse when it is down. This mystical fog is the taste of success, adrenaline, and dopamine rush, which pulls them deeper and deeper until one is addicted.

Making this fog thicker, there is too much liquid money for some people, especially investors. They are hungry to get richer, so they invest sometimes almost blindly in every project they feel slightly better than nonsense. Governments also support this kind of ~innovation~, but on their level, investments are just KPIs and checkboxes, in a quantitative, but unfortunately not a qualitative way.

In the end, there are new startup competitions every day, hackathons, accelerators, and investors on literally every corner, but somehow the innovation much sought after won't show up that often. This is a large topic worth another book to be written about. Long story short: If the framework and best practices are present, the ecosystem is supportive, there are increasing pools of mentors with knowledge and experience, capital is nearly endless, there are problems to solve, and startups are the only piece of the puzzle where the fit is not 100% complete, then we should see a towering pile of innovative products and services.

Why is that not the case? Anyway, another topic for another book.

These and similar insights motivated us to write this book for you. We, the two authors of this book, have different stories. One has a business background with thousands of customer development interviews and product-market fit exploration, the other has a more industrial one, involving engineering, quality assurance, and manufacturing. We met in the Hungarian start-up community, both interested in tech, innovation, behavioral economics, became friends, and started supporting each other. Both of us are mentoring startups actively, focusing especially on hardware startups. Hardware startups, because they do not get the support they deserve.

Building hardware is still not that sexy for most people as we know, but still, there are heroes out there, who are brave/crazy enough to start a hardware business. They are like legendary pioneers who are the first ones to step into the unknown, which could soon be Mars. They know that they only have one chance. Everything has to fit for the first or nearly the first time. They are like adventurers, pioneers on a treasure hunt, looking for extreme uncertainty. There is only one route, one goal, and a limited opportunity window. There is a big chance of failure, and of course, the existence of the treasure is not certain either.

Hardware makes every journey unique and specific. This is a difficult path to walk on. We have often been the tour guides on this journey, from green tech battery solutions to sports equipment and 3D printing projects, from ideas to product development and production kickoffs while also having seen many more projects fail due to many reasons we will target here later.

We cannot reach out to everyone in person, so we have tried to summarize our experiences in the book you are holding in your hands or reading on your screen.

We offer you some value here, let's have a look!
You are at chapter **#2** at the moment. The following chapters are structured as follows.

#3 – At first, we collect the main influencing factors, why so many startups fail. It is important to have a general common understanding. We start with the root cause of all problems, then we move to general problems and discuss the hardware-specific problems at the end.

#4 – Second, we analyze the lean startup method as one of the best currently existing frameworks. We summarize the origin, the past, and the future of this framework.
As a next step, we continue in chapter **#5** with possibilities on how to find a better-fitting framework. These two chapters are one unit, building the base of our framework.

The next big unit consists of chapters **#6-#8**. We will introduce the building blocks of complexity and delve deeper and deeper into the topics until we are able to plan individual roadmaps. With this ability to create roadmaps, the new framework, and the tools currently available, almost everything will be there, ready for success!
#6 – We define the base layers.
#7 – We start digging deeper in complexity.
#8 – Together we learn how to edit the roadmap to any project.

#9 – This Chapter is a brief summary of how to not only survive but win the hardware startup journey.

#10 – We give you even more ammunition, like further suggestions on resources, potential partners we value, etc.

#11 – A few words about us, the authors, and our main projects.

#12 – Acknowledgements to good humans.

Life is a two-way street. We got great support from other humans, now it is our turn to give back to the world by writing this book and providing further support.

#3 Why HW startups fail

Startups fell, fall, and will fall.

This is an eternal truth, not just for startups, but for all companies, at least as long as capitalism rules the markets. Acquiring a share on the free market is comparable to surviving in the wilderness – even though it looks less savage at first glance, the level of cruelty could very well be the same.

We are not even close to David Attenborough's narrative style, but the scene resembles the journey of newborn turtles reaching the sea, a grand passage filled with obstacles, though much safer than the final destination, where new, different threats await. Their only chance is the mixture of instinct and luck. Startups are better shielded due to the knowledge and external support, but still, as you can see in the infographic below, only a small proportion of them survive the first wave of obstacles.

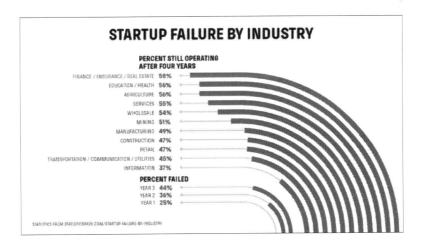

STARTUP FAILURE BY INDUSTRY

PERCENT STILL OPERATING
AFTER FOUR YEARS

FINANCE / INSURANCE / REAL ESTATE **58%**
EDUCATION / HEALTH **56%**
AGRICULTURE **56%**
SERVICES **55%**
WHOLESALE **54%**
MINING **51%**
MANUFACTURING **49%**
CONSTRUCTION **47%**
RETAIL **47%**
TRANSPORTATION / COMMUNICATION / UTILITIES **45%**
INFORMATION **37%**

PERCENT FAILED
YEAR 3 **44%**
YEAR 2 **36%**
YEAR 1 **25%**

STATISTICS FROM STATISTICBRAIN.COM/STARTUP-FAILURE-BY-INDUSTRY

There are numerous other factors besides good luck and intuition, that can determine whether a startup is going to survive in the long run. We will approach this topic on three levels, trying to find answers to what is behind so many unsuccessful (hardware) startups.

The first level of factors is the **original sin**, the most fundamental of all problems and issues: the human brain itself. We live in the same reality, but what we see, how detailed we see it, and how we process the information is different for all of us. This forms the base of our existence, helps us understand what happens around us, what may kill us, and what supports our survival. Understanding helps us make decisions. Good decisions bring us to our desired goals, and to reach these goals, we need to be consistent, progressive, and have a good work ethic.

The second level is the topic of **general problems and misunderstandings that** can happen to all starting and growing businesses, not only startups. We all solve problems day in and day out. We can offer good or bad solutions to existing or non-existing problems. We may target the wrong customers or simply set the price too high or low. We can also try to outsmart our customers, competitors or the whole world. Based on the original sin, we collect the most typical problems, similar to the ones we listed above.

On the third level, there are the **hardware startup-specific causes**, which we present to you with the help of dummy stories to show a realistic picture of the obstacles startups face. We aim to provide you with an overview of the pitfalls to avoid and potential paths you can take, adding some thoughts alongside the case studies as well.

#3·1 Level 1 — The original sin

It might be too theatrical, but we believe there are not too many fundamental issues that make HW startups fail, just various forms of similar problems pushing the emerging companies down the slope. Calling these the 'original sin' means that they are the real core of most of the problems that HW startups face. Okay, but what is the original sin? – you might ask. It is the way our brain works, the thoughts and processes – mostly subconscious – that are supposed to help us, but this help may be rather a disadvantage sometimes.

You probably know that some of the processes in our brains are nature-, while many nurture-type functions; meaning we own some since the moment we were born, while many behavior patterns we learn from our parents, in school, from friends, at workplaces and so on. This compound of mental wiring, processes, and shortcuts makes us who we are. It evolved with us, sometimes making things easy, but sometimes difficult by causing a multitude of problems often remaining unseen, untargeted.

So, what is behind all those issues? It's no magic. Wrong decisions and, more precisely, defective decision-making processes, are caused by problems in three main areas, or as we call them, the three "A"s: **Awareness**, **Approach,** and **Action**. The basic traits we were born with and the things we learn throughout our lives shape our decision-making process. Each moment generates so much information, not even a supercomputer can handle it and this incredible amount of sensory and cognitive data is processed consciously and subconsciously by our brains every single second.

To be able to cope with all this, our brain has a simplified model of functioning:

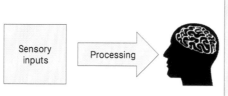

1. Are we in danger?
2. If yes: Fight, Freeze or Flee
3. If no: What does this remind me on? (--> Looking of patterns in the memories)
4. Ok, I think this will happen: ...
5. Is it what happened?
6. No: What happened and why? What should we react?
7. Reaction
8. Storing new pattern, refining existing ones when there is no danger.

This is, of course, an oversimplification of the matter, but for now, it is sufficient to see how decision making works. In the following we are going to see that our perception of reality is distorted in many ways, which can be described by malfunctions or sometimes just unhelpful patterns in the three "A"s – and this is what creates the original sin, leading us to wrong decisions.

Every situation can be traced back to at least one of these three elements: **Awareness, Approach,** and **Action**. When building a product from scratch, this is more important than we can imagine, especially in the case of hardware products, where the complexity grows exponentially.

Think of this situation like a computer, where Awareness is the hardware and the embedded software, while Approach is the core of the Operating System, with Action being the front-end and the User Interface present to us from the outside. There may be cases where the team has more than one fundamental issue. Having troubles with all three means no good. Let's investigate these areas one by one!

#3·1·1 A1 — Awareness

"The quality or state of being aware: knowledge and understanding that something is happening or exists"

Since the dawn of mankind, it has always been important to understand the environment surrounding us. It is important to distinguish between food, poison, potential prey, and dangerous animals, and to understand the ongoing processes of life. Our brains were made for this kind of work. There are different types of sensory input that our brain processes and builds a library of information to create memories and patterns to help us survive and reproduce. Speed of processing is the key. It was crucial 10 000 years ago, and it still is today. Our brains are constantly running evaluation- and bias systems to help us survive. Things we have once learned will help us in the future, but only if we are able to deduce the right conclusions from the information at hand. This system is called the cognitive bias codex and the image below shows its complexity.

On one hand, this cognitive bias helps us make decisions faster, but on the other hand, it also limits us, since our brains prefer the familiar paths over the unknown ones. As a result, we often fail to critically evaluate the information provided by a friend, relative, or any other person we regard as trustworthy. We also believe 'facts' more easily when told by someone owning a professor's or doctor's title. We also prefer products we see more often or have a certain color, form, or smell, that are more fa-

THE COGNITIVE BIAS CODEX

Too Much Information

Not Enough Meaning

What Should We Remember?

Need To Act Fast

miliar to us from past experiences. To put it short, our brains manipulate us to make decisions in an energy-efficient way. Too much thinking is slow, and the predator may hide behind any bush, ready to attack.

We do not realize that we do not think through every situation individually, when facing it; it takes a lot of time and effort to develop this kind of awareness. A good example of this is when you have a great idea and wonder why no one has ever done it before. Most probably, there is a very good reason that you are not aware of. Your brain tells you 'good job, very nice work, you are a genius'. With every thought you are more convinced that your idea is brilliant, and critical thinking is switched off due to the dopamine rush. The next day you explain your genius idea to a friend, family member, colleague, or anyone within reach and the harsh reality slaps you in the face: you have not considered many factors that will likely render your idea worthless.

We are also unaware of the patterns we have been learning since birth, even though these define us and set us apart from others in many ways. This is a key component of awareness: self-awareness, or in other words, knowing our characteristics and the unique elements of our personality. Understanding how we function is important, but understanding that most people function similarly, but not in the same way is even more im-portant in case you are building a product not just for yourself. Finding the patterns in the similarities and differences between people – ourselves included – may be the key to success.

The competence to make decisions is called situational awareness or situation awareness. This is the awareness of environmental elements and events around you in time and space, what they mean, why they are there and how they affect your business now and in the future. Another factor of awareness is the range of awareness of the external environment: the things that exist and happen in the world in the past, present and future. The limit here is the processing capacity of the human brain; knowledge, perception and experience. Think of the information that is stored and processed in the brain as a funnel: it has a width or radius and a depth, as you can see in the drawing below.

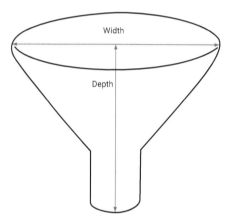

Depth is the knowledge and experience of a particular subject, and width is the range of the connected topics, problems, phenomena you are aware of. There are funnels that are deeper than wide, and there are wide ones being rather shallow. You need to learn, train and practice to increase the volume of your funnel and to build new funnels, because you cannot take the things you do not see, feel, or know that you should into account, when making decisions.

As you can see, our brains try to look for similar patterns in our stored database; and we try to apply the same things over and over again in different situations with a little fine tuning – which could be helpful, but may sometimes lead us down the wrong path, especially in business. If you have sold cookies or ran a lemonade stand before, it does not mean you can sell a B2B SW solution to manufacturing companies as well. Complexity and diversity make the game hard. Being unaware of them or oversimplifying things may result in inaccurate business plans, malfunctioning processes, or sometimes even useless products. If we are not humble enough to admit our limitations, we can make false assumptions, false predictions, and, after a heavy punch in the stomach from life, we will still fail to understand what went wrong.

When we are aware of ourselves and our environment, we can filter the things around us, but these filters will also determine the blind spots, the things we do not see. This is why a trusted team is really important. More people with different filters and blind spots can assess the situation more efficiently and make better decisions both in the short and long term.

There is a typical type of event among startup ecosystem entities called hackathon, where new ideas receive the most awareness. Experienced professionals of various areas are invited to form a jury and evaluate different business ideas of future startuppers. This is rather a great opportunity to test your level of awareness. If you use this opportunity and the professional advice right, you can find the areas where you lack understanding, such as the market, your skills, or customer needs, which deficiencies might cause you a headache later on.

Expand your awareness by reading and learning. The more you know, the more you understand. The more you understand about people, markets, processes, dynamics, logic and consequences of the field you operate in, the better strategy you can form to be prepared for whatever comes. Keep one eye on the current situation and the other one on the long term goal to make sure you are on the right track. This will lead you to your goal through constant refinement, replanning and avoiding traps, because you will see what to do and what not. Being alert and walking with open eyes and ears is not enough. This is a journey of thousands of miles, which starts with one step – self awareness – which you can slowly extend to your environment, your business and the entire market, to become the basis of your approach and attitude.

If you pause for a moment you will realize that this is training for an infinite game. There is no goal to reach, there is no all-time winner, just continuous learning, practice, and development. Developing your awareness helps you make better decisions by seeing and understanding more factors inside and outside the project. To be able to react in time in the right manner, never let your guard down, and stay frosty!

#3·1·2 A2 – Approach

"The taking of preliminary steps toward a particular purpose"

Now that we have got hold of the things we understand, and also of those we do not, the next step is to use our awareness to make a system, a machine that will help us achieve our goal. We need this system to have the right approach to processing situations, identifying problems, and finding solutions in an efficient way.

OK, but what exactly is the definition of approach?
Coming closer. Not just physically but also mentally. If we see a task, an obstacle, or a problem, first we see it from a distance. We may understand what is happening, but not the root cause. What we understand may also be refined during the process of approximating the problem or task. We collect information, find the patterns, understand the whys and hows sooner or later, and with the total picture in our head, we may finally think of the actions we should perform. Since we need to reuse this method frequently, it needs to be systematic, measurable and repeatable. To sum it up, approach is the process of gathering data to understand and plan the action we think is the most appropriate in the different situations. This way, we are able to create processes and predict the end results with repeatable accuracy.

Without a proper approach, the whole game we play – no matter if we consider life as a whole or just a small project – is nothing but guesswork. Without a system to look at things people would be running blind, without control and an understanding of the processes and the possible outcomes. This is what everybody tries to avoid. People who blame bad luck and external factors for not succeeding or not getting the desired results, often simply do not have the right approach to the things they would like to achieve.

Whatever role you have at the moment in your project or at home, protocols, routines and processes are around us and keep us safe from insanity. You do not forget how and when to brush your teeth, how to make a cup of coffee and you know when to pay bills. As for your job, you know when and how to pay taxes, you know what the steps of setting up an email account are, you know how the printer works, and how to scan an invoice. What would happen if we had to figure out what to do every moment? We would waste a lot of time and energy making every single decision. We cannot 'afford' that and neither can any organization.

The approach is good if it is like a scientific experiment: repeatable and reproducible. This means that anybody should be able to make it and receive the same quality of output at the end anytime. This is how one can create manuals to help people operate machines, perform tasks and solve problems. And this is why if you find an unplanned function or malfunction in the prototype of the product you are developing, you need to stop and go through the mental protocol of how you got here before you take everything apart: to find out, why is it working like it does and what you are going to need to fix it. These protocols are critical, especially to refine them until the approach is right.

Experience and repeatability of tasks make processes, processes make protocols, protocols make routines, routines make systems and systems make operations. Operations serve goals and deliver the results we want to achieve. Your approach makes this happen. Your approach will be judged based on how well you can define the smallest valuable logical steps. The most important criterion, however, will be how well you can link these logical steps together and forge a kick-ass strategy.

At school you can learn almost everything you need to improve your logical thinking, serving as a good soil for developing the right approach later on. However, this does not mean you are lost, if, as an adult, you still feel you need some improvement.

Games improving logic may come in various forms, from board games to puzzles, online and offline, played with friends, family or alone, which are equally helpful to become better in building strategy and approaching problems.

Another important factor is curiosity, the urge to understand things, especially why and how they work. A child taking things apart and trying to reassemble them is going to improve in terms of assembly and will also understand the way things work. But then again, you do not have to be a child to discover: people never stop learning, and you can start to look into things at any age, which is going to form not only your approach, but also widen your awareness. Logic and curiosity together form the drive to develop a good approach. To build processes from scratch or reverse-engineer existing ones, you will not need more than that..

#3·1·3 A3 – Action

'the fact or process of doing something, typically to achieve an aim'

Besides **how** you do things and what is going on in your mind, we are also going to involve **what** you actually do and should do.

Does your personal behavior influence the success of a start-up?

Yes, absolutely. More than you think. Your level of motivation, work ethic, respect for others, and temper are all important parts of the game. Action, along with awareness and approach make culture. A good culture almost always wins, while toxic ones are going to be weeded out sooner or later. If you elevate others, the potential output may reach stellar heights, toxicity on the other hand will drastically decrease the efficiency of the whole team, and this is not even the gravest scenario that may happen.

When it comes to action, things can go wrong very easily in just a blink of an eye, but you need to have two main aims in focus all the time: achieve the goals and keep good people on board. Let us assume your approach is good and your next step is the execution of the plan. If you do not act the way you should, a plan is going to remain as it is: just a plan. How can you fix this?

First: work on your self awareness, ask for external help, in a professional form, e.g. a coach, and have some people around whom you trust, and who dare to be radically transparent with you. **Second**, be humble, empathic, and human. **Third**: admit your mistakes, ask for understanding and show your best in willing to change. And **last, but not least**: Build resilience!

You are the impersonation of the startup, your culture will be the culture of the team. You are like a parent to your team. Your attitude, mentality, motivation and dedication is the glue keeping the pieces together. Use it wisely, it is a powerful tool.

Key takeaways

- A1 – Take time and energy to analyze your own filters and blind spots! Know yourself! Meditate!
- A1 – Try to be objective in decision making and involve others to help discover your blind spots! Know the situation!
- A1 – Be like a chess grandmaster, expand your awareness of the possible options and prepare your next moves! Know your possibilities!
- A2 – You need a system for the way to approach every problem and task, resembling a perfectly engineered machine.
- A2 – Poor or slow decisions can kill a project.
- A2 – Build on your awareness!
- A2 – Try to automate everything you can!
- A3 – You are the startup, the startup is you. Every step of yours is crucial. Your motivation, your dedication, your deeds will determine the culture of your team.
- A3 – Build up your resilience, be humble, be human!

#3·2 Level 2 – General problems

Even if someone has developed high levels in the three "A"s, there are numerous further reasons why startups could fail. Anyone may take a wrong step or head in a completely wrong direction, but these are not fatal mistakes destroying any project – at least not alone. Series of wrong decisions are. Some of these decisions are field-specific, while others more general. In this chapter we will target the general, non-field-specific problems; a widely studied topic, which you can find countless articles, videos, and books about, providing you with a deep understanding of the different factors. Here we are going to summarize our thoughts on only three factors, which we regard as the most important ones:

- Founder issues
- Validation and product-market fit
- Execution of the plan

As we are alway seeking to find the root cause of every issue, we have chosen these three problems, as root causes. Alway try to find the root cause. Otherwise you will cure the symptom, but not the original disease.

Every startup starts with an idea of a founder or founders. This is why we will also start with the issues that can pop up.

The first big mission of startups is to validate the idea, form a product out of it, and find the product-market fit, which will be the second topic, why startups fail.

During the development of the product, there are more and more tasks to do, focus has to be like a laser beam, and productivity should be over 100%. The afternoon sessions slowly turn into a company-like operation. Many fail to do so, what we will discuss as execution issues.

#3·2·1 Founder issues

It is almost impossible to start a startup alone. Even if you are talented, you cannot have all the competencies necessary to start a business, especially as big as founders usually dream of. This is why in most of the cases we are talking about founders, in plural form. However, starting a journey in a startup together does not only mean sharing knowledge and experience, it also means sharing the risk. It forms a relationship based on trust, common goals, vision and maybe even a mission. It literally resembles a relationship, more like marriage, than a one night stand, since you do everything together, share both laughter and crying. Sadly, too many stories end with crying.

When it comes to problems, ego is the first we need to talk about, and I immediately suggest you read *Ego is the enemy* by Ryan Holiday. I am convinced this is one of the biggest threats for startups. A CEO with high ego can represent poor self-awareness, and a bad attitude. They are easily offended and they know everything better. What could be more toxic? This is one of the reasons why many startuppers quit or teams break up after their first hackathon. It is easy to be offended by the criticism, but it is wise to learn why you did not see the same weak points as the jury did. But also in daily life, two high-ego founders tend to argue like children in kindergarten: just emotions, no rationality. One of the worst traits of a founder is to have emotional overreaction when you need a cold head. This can be stressful for the founders and also for the whole team. In this case the cofounders take too much conflict, which can paralyze even the most simple decision-making processes. However, the opposite could be equally harmful for the success of a startup: not taking conflicts can ruin any good project by preventing the exploration of the best possible solutions.

Another problem causing the failure of numerous startups are the founders overestimating themselves. This issue can be identified the most easily via risk taking. You should be bold, but not insane. Taking too much risk may be an ego problem, but this can also be traced back to something else: low level of awareness. Not knowing or not taking the environment and the external factors into account does not protect the startup being subject to them; thus taking too high risk because of not being aware of it may take the project down the slope all the same. Just like in the previous case, the opposite is not a good option either: starting a business will be risky in any case. If you cannot take it, probably this is not the right track for you. Too high a level of risk-aversion is one of the main reasons for investors and financial experts to restrain progress so often: they usually have a more conservative attitude towards risk taking than founders do.

Bias may be harmful in another way as well: overestimating the effort your people, especially co-founders, will put into the cause. In many cases the father of the idea gives his heart and soul to achieve the goals, while co-founders who do not feel the project their own, just work to windward, without really putting their best into it. It is even worse, when a cofounder is an old friend. Seeing your friend ruining your dream is one of the worst experiences a startupper may face. It is a terrible feeling, even though it is rarely the whole story. It takes two to tango.

We can often hear about startup CEO-s and founders living like rock stars. They travel from event to event, they present killer pitches, own fancy offices and high-end notebooks, but their product never actually reaches the market. This is an addiction to fame, which takes them far away from reality. It is easier to be in the spotlight, than to stay humble and work hard with your team, who are at home trying to fulfill the impossible mission. If at least one founder has this way of living, the startup is already in danger and definitely not on the way to success. This is a sad but not rare scenario.

If you think it through thoroughly, you can see a pattern in every founder issue. No extremes are good, both ends of the scale are dangerous, so you need to find a balance in every situation, which requires a minimum high level at the three "A"s as well. This is a risky game with a lot of different stressors, as you may have already recognized, where you risk basically everything you have, including your relationship, health, family and wealth.

To handle all these challenges of being a founder of a startup, you need to build up resilience. Many founders break during this journey, making their dreams and startup sink with them. It is hard to keep a rational level of risk taking and resilience, we know. The first – and most important – factor is to improve and monitor yourself constantly. Before criticizing the co-founders and the team members, make sure that you as a founder do not fall into any of these traps. Once confident you do not commit the common founder mistakes, you can turn your eyes on your team members to make sure that you, as an entity form a cooperative, productive unit.

Communication is the first thing to get right. Systematicity and radical transparency are the key, which is well-discussed in the book Principles by Ray Dalio. It is important to have the goals and performance expectations set clear from the very beginning. The best solution is to have them written down (less like a marriage in most parts of the world, but safe for all parties). It does not have to be a contract, a single job description or an agreement can be a great help in situations, when the cofounders cannot get along anymore. You need to be able to speak up for yourself, and tell others how you feel and what you think – but always keep the purpose of making a great product or service in mind. Remember, personal interest is secondary, even though this is often more than challenging.

In mathematics 1+1=3 means you are dumb, but in teamwork it means synergy. If the founders can work together well, they can even achieve the impossible. It is alright to fight, it is alright to argue – if it is for the startup, for the greater good, and not for the individual and the ego. Passion is important. Trust is also important, so is empathy, kicka** work ethic, and diversity. This is what makes a good founder team. It is, once again, like marriage. Finding your partner for life is only one part, keeping the fire alive is another – and often the harder.

#3·2·2 Validation and Product-Market Fit

Validation is a little bit vague and quite often it is not specific enough. You should validate. There is a lot of talk concerning how you should do validation, and the list of tools is also quite long: 'Mom-test', interviews, surveys, whatever the startuppers may think of. It is important to know them, however the key to doing validation right, or at least better than most of the startups, is defining the measurable key indicators of validation. In the book *Measure what matters* by John Doerr you can find many useful insights for that. Why, and what should I validate, and how this will help me build my business? This is one of the most important questions that should be considered in the idea and development phase.

Early-stage startups have almost nothing in common with established companies, especially when it comes to bringing innovations to market. They have no historical data, mostly no real brand equity, no previous brand promises and no marketing budget to create global 'brainwash' type campaigns. For better or worse, they have no clear scheme to follow, or fundamentals to build upon.

The way Microsoft or Apple can bring a product to market is very different from the way a startup does. Microsoft can afford failures, can spend 50-100 million in marketing budget, can hire influencers, and so on. They cannot, however, test products with real customers or run their innovation processes the real lean-startup-way, as the brand permeates the whole process and they have to be secretive to maintain a competitive advantage over their competitors. Established brands have already made prom-ises, so customers have associations in their minds describing those brands and their relation to everything they have to offer. In this regard, startups resemble a tabula rasa, starting their journey on square one. A blank sheet of paper on which they write their promises they will have to keep later on. Let us give a brief example! In a moment of brilliance a genius idea pops into your head and you want to create a startup. In your mind you have already burned the wealth of a smaller country, but something stops you for a moment. Is it really a genius idea? What should I do to find out? → This is called validation.

Customer needs + Solution + Business model = Money (ex-change for the value you provide)

Customer needs ≠ You think you know what your customer needs. In real life – at the beginning – it is just an assumption made by you, just guesswork, nothing else.

Customer needs = You 'go out of the building' and ask your customers what their problem is and they will most probably tell you what they are looking for in a potential solution they would like to sell for.

*: Thank you Steve Blank

Founders of startups often mix up the problem, value and solution. They create a problem statement, which they think people have and believe that the solution is validated just to figure out later that no one is interested in their solution, since it is not a real problem, the the offer meaning no value to people at all or even though it does, the solution might not be the right one, so is not well received among customers. It can be brilliant in your mind, but it may simply be a non-existent problem that you would like to solve. To have people go all crazy over your goods and services you either need hype or a problem. Creating hype is a different story, so now let's focus on the onset of success: people having problems and you knowing the problems that matter to them. Do you have the right solution for the right segment of customers, solving their existing problem in a way they are willing to pay for? If the answer to any part of this question is weak, you will get a headache all too soon.

In case you are selling a "smart mug", the use cases might be plenty: showing the temperature so children do not burn their mouths and parents can stay relaxed; helping a coffee or tea enthusiast make sure that the beverage is consumed just at the right temperature; or a person on a special diet being able to track consumption. Your mug might be able to solve all these problems, but which is the one causing distress to people at all? Are these real problems, the solution of which brings value to the life of people, or just the products of your imagination? Unveil the answer to these questions, and you might just have found yourself a gold mine.

The scope of problem validation can help you understand whether people actually struggle with the problem you are trying to solve, and more importantly or better said, from all the different issues your offer is able to solve, which is the problem that matters the most. Problem validation is no more and no less than what the phrase implies: validation of the problem. Just the problem. You need to be able to prioritize the problems you are trying to solve and understand that you need to make decisions about where to allocate resources, which customer segment to listen to when collecting feedback or sorting emails or signups.

Being able to separate the different use cases, you can run tests to understand how the conversion is going to happen and what the price of access to the potential customers is. At this point you are not validating the value (promise) or the solution itself. Your scope is just the size of the potential market, the conversion numbers for different acquisition channels and the price of 'acquisition'.

Once you understand the scope of the problem, you can start to examine and explore the current solutions and the value people have or miss from the current solutions. You have to remember that there is a solution to all problems. Maybe not the best one or probably not a competitive product, but when people have a problem, they will look for solutions. After you get the validation right, you will find that your product or service is better and more tailored to your customers' needs after each validation and optimization cycle. When you reach the 'optimum', it is called the product-market fit. PMF is the holy grail(?) of a successful business.

Exceptions: market-maker products will create a demand for a new solution that has not existed before. There are ways to uncover such latent needs, but that is beyond the capacity of this book and we would become entangled in behavioral science just by trying to cover the basics. Take our word for it: it is possible, but extremely complicated. Market-makers are more often than not the exception rather than the rule.

#3·2·3 Execution of the plan

Founder issues resolved, validation mindset understood, product-market fit clear – there is only one unanswered question remaining: how to get it done. Getting the theory right is one thing, but as the old Latin proverb goes: 'facta, non verba'. You will always be judged by your actions, and your product, not by a theoretical startup quiz score.

Even the best idea, the best vision can fail on many levels, due to mistakes in the execution process.

- **Wrong focus** is the biggest threat. You work over 70 hours a week and so does your team, but you focus on the easy tasks instead of the important ones, since they give you the illusion of progress. I had the same problem in my startup at the beginning. I tried to follow the 100h work-week, reaching 86h at max, but the focus was not right. I solved a lot of issues, but not the most important ones.
- **Failing to measure progress OR measuring the wrong things** can lead you down the wrong alley. Which processes should be measured and how? What are the results you may consider good? Are you measuring the

right thing? KPIs (key performance indicators) may look good, yet somehow the bank account is still empty. This can mean various things: your KPIs might not be the right ones, you could measure them the wrong way, the plan may be wrong, or you might have underestimated the costs.

- **Failure in team management: accountability and transparency.**
- Since you have a limited amount of time and money, you need to focus on the tasks of highest priority. You need to deal with them quickly, yet properly. How do you measure that? How do you hold your team accountable if you do not possess that particular domain knowledge? What if your best worker resigns? How should you handle problems in team dynamics? Poor answers to these questions can be as deadly as wounds in the long run.
- **Under- or overestimating the size of the project** are both misleading. You think you will validate and develop a product in 6 months to acquire investment? Good luck! You think you need 2 years for a proper product? Who will feed the team in the meantime? Time/cost to market can use up all the resources.
- **Time and/or location** can also kill a startup. Startups are meant to be global, but most of the startups start local. On one hand, this could be a threat. On the other hand, where else should they start, except for online businesses? Even if 100% online, location independent startups can fail due to timing too, being too early or too late. Sometimes customers are not ready yet, or there is a key technology missing, so you are too early. But the opposite can also happen, when the market is already saturated, and the market entry is not worth it.

- **Wrong hiring strategy** may bring the fall. There are usually two main problems. You either need more people and hire anyone you can, just to grow, and try to help them grow with the startup; or you hire the rockstars, who have the knowledge and experience you are missing and you try to put up with them even if they have a toxic personality, just to achieve the growth. There is a golden rule: hire slow, fire fast. Keep this in mind!
- **Finances getting chaotic**, casburn rate too high, lack of professional operation in sense of financial discipline – these and numerous other financial mistakes can take you to a point, where the bank account is so empty, that no more pivots are possible, and the operation has to be terminated.

As you can see, all the general problems are either Awareness, Approach or Action problems. Now it is time to focus on hardware-specific problems too, but of course, the original sin and its effects are going to stay with us in the next pages.

#3·3 Level 3 – Specific problems

Besides the regular challenges, hardware startups have some special problems to deal with, which we separated into three main categories.

The first type are the problems occurring from founders thinking a HW startup is a SW startup, just a little bit more special. Not a big deal, just buying some stuff from Ebay or Aliexpress and assembling it into something. Hilarious, but very often this is the case.

The second issue is the missing engineering competency. There is a general misconception that you may lead a HW startup without being familiar with several areas of engineering. You may start a startup without proper coding knowledge, but you cannot develop a physical product without considering all the important topics, such as user-safety, quality, production efficiency, choice of material and processes, and parameters of the machines used.

Last, but not least: we have been building cars for over 100 years and other products for over 200 years now. Experiences of these years have often turned into rules carved in stone. Startups may be disruptive, but in most of the cases changing the industry standards completely is not going to work. Without knowing and accepting all the rules already existing, while other players set extra for/against you, it is hard to step in and try to set new rules. Startups are like Davids against Goliaths. The big players will not trust you, and will not even consider you as a serious player on the market, until you are powerful enough to be considered. This is our third category: the cases where the status quo is under attack.

#3·3·1 Problems occurring from differences between SW and HW

'Think big. Start small. Scale fast.' – says literally every startup consultant.

We have learned through the success of many non-HW startups that this mentality may bring victory for them, but this does not mean it fits the HW environment as well, since we have already highlighted many thoughts on why HW startups are different.

Hardware startups are not even startups in the classical way. They are rather 'just' emerging companies intending to innovate the product development cycle and the way to mass production. Their path is more like a rapid evolution from startup to engineering office, then to manufacturing and assembly company at the end. The transition may be fast, but it is still there and cannot be skipped. And this is the biggest mistake one can make: living in an illusion of being a "real" startup and not moving further.

SW startups often think in sprints and short time periods, when it comes to development cycles. This, however, is not going to work in HW product development, due to several reasons:

- **Lead time of component- and material sourcing** takes time. For some critical components this lead time may be longer than a year. You can sometimes buy with a shorter lead time too by finding a kind distributor having stocks for sale, but it is usually inversely proportional with the price.
- **Period of testing and validation** is often not part of the time plan – a factor, which, again, cannot be skipped to be able to move further, and which changes the scheduling compared to SW startups a lot. Missing this from the time plan is even more risky, as in most of the cases you do not even do it yourself, but there is a third party involved, e.g. a certification body for transport, and safety tests.
- **Development of parts, assemblies, packaging, and product** also take time. You are bound to design a prod-

uct that can be produced, assembled, and also complies with a set of requirements, which cannot be done from one day to another.

- The **result of the development** cannot be a product with less than 100% readiness. You update a SW frequently, but you cannot update HW so easily.
- **Capacity of the supply chain** is also different. You not only have subcontractors, who can adapt overnight if necessary, but also suppliers and distributors, who need to cross-check and cooperate with manufacturers and real subsuppliers of special technologies, which makes the whole process way more complex.
- **Investments** in HW startups are high, measured both in financial investment and in considering other resources, such as knowledge. In SW startups you buy equipment to help you code and store and run the code, but for HW startups everything is more physical. Machines, assembly lines, and the storage of materials, parts and finished goods take space and – of course – money. An automated assembly line can literally cost millions in any currency. Every special technology costs money, time to deliver, time to set up, and staff to operate.

#3·3·2 Issues based on lack of competency

Startups have always meant rapid learning, development, and scaling. For SW startups it is not impossible to find employees with some level of the desired competency, even though the labor costs are high. You need developers, testers, devops, quality, scrum master, product owner, and the rest is – exaggerated – not a big deal.

Compared to that, developing a HW product is SW, plus

- Mechanical development engineers
- HW development electrical engineers
- Embedded SW developers
- Process engineers
- Design engineers
- Quality engineers
- Test engineers
- Validation engineers
- Logistic experts
- Purchasing experts
- etc.

Even if you have all the staff there, the level of knowledge and experience also matters. There are tips and tricks you can only learn during 10+ years experience on the field. A freshman will not automatically know the right wall-thickness of plastic, or realize if it is totally no go, nor will they know which parameters should be set up on the milling machine to get the right surface quality immediately.

Startups we have seen so far have often made mistakes in this area, which is totally understandable. Working for a startup might be sexy and appealing for a young person, but not so much for an industry expert having 15+ years of experience, family, children, and possibly low tolerance in risk taking. They live a good and stable life, why would they jump on a volatile and insecure train? What can be a good deal for them here? ESO (employee stock option), or something similar may be an option, but from financial stability and capital perspective startups are often not the best bet.

Remaining on financial topics, most of the startups cannot afford senior engineers in the number the complexity of the product would require. Starting with juniors may be cheap, but in the end this is the more expensive way – even though investing in the development of your people always pays off after a while.

#3·3·3 Industry standards 'non-compatible' with startups and supply chain issues

There is a 'generation' gap between HW startups and traditional manufacturing and assembly companies. Corporations and startups speak different languages, have different expectations, and their processes also differ in numerous aspects. The instant scaling from brainstorming party to a production company is the biggest challenge of building hardware products needing diverse and numerous competencies to develop. This process is really challenging to lead or even build up in a short time. Doing this in a very conservative and excluding environment makes it more difficult.

Long-standing companies cannot compete with startups in speed, but why should they? It is their playground. They have made the rules (together with governments and other organizations), so, as a startup, you need to compete with them, facing challenges, such as:

- **No financial trust**, if you are not profitable and do not have at least 3 closed full years. You may get conditions impossible to meet and extremely strict contracts.
- **Payment terms are hard** to live with as a startup, due to cash flow difficulties. You are expected to pay in advance,

as you do not have the financial stability, but your big customers pay you in 90 days, from the end of month.
- **Slow and long processes** and decision making due to bureaucracy and numerous stakeholders.
- **Suppliers will prioritize huge-volume customers** over you.
- Almost **nobody gives you free support**, because all the companies are pushed to their limits to serve the market.
- **Other engineers will not take you seriously,** considering you as a child from the playground having a cute idea rather than a partner in any way.

This is a tough situation. Nobody among the giants on the market is going to hold out a helping hand to startups. They will not even watch you. They will just wait until you grow up to match them or disappear. This mentality is completely wrong and has made many numerous companies fall, but unfortunately this is still the status quo.

#3·3·4 Case studies

It is always sad to hear about the failure of interesting projects, no matter if it was a startup or not. Where physical startups most often fail is the first contact with the customers, still in the prototype phase. Here we lose the majority of them already, due to improper validation, financial issues, or founder issues.

Remaining startups building a hardware product may be divided into two groups. The first group contains really good products that reach the market on their own, and the second group contains projects we would love to see alive and our love keeps them alive for a while until there is no more hope, no more room for a pivot. We are experienced supporters on Kickstarter, a platform, which unfortunately has a long history of 'success-fully backed, yet destined to fail' projects. This is the second group of surviving startups. Of course, this is not the only way, but it helps us understand the harsh reality, that just a small number of products reach the customers.

On the other hand, we have also supported and/or took part in projects, where a startup was based on a good idea, even had an MVP or a working prototype, yet had a hard time hitting further milestones. Too many project-failures are caused by the underestimation of complexity, time, effort, and other crucial steps lying between an idea and selling your product to real customers. Without understanding the must-have components for building a startup, you have no chance. Even without hardcore developer skills, you can build succesful SW startups, but with hardware you have no chance without experience and knowing all the technologies involved to a certain level, which often means 5+ years of learning and gaining experience.

Let's see some imaginary stories, where we can show the most common traps and explain them. All the stories are fictional, based on the mix of some failed projects we know. For a better understanding, we have artificially organized the problems and created a deadly mix of them to show you some examples on what could go wrong.

#3·3·5 Case 1 — Crowdfounding and FarEast OxM

A small group of young industrial design engineers have an idea to make a minimalistic backpack with built-in tech gadgets, a bluetooth speaker and a location tracker. They make some cool prototypes and after a successful crowdfunding campaign they fail to deliver. Updates are not coming, backers are frustrated. What went wrong? Let's check it step by step!

The idea comes from a group of friends, who studied industrial design together. They go through the design and planning process and make a prototype. This is what they have studied and also what most of them do as a dayjob. They decide to make it happen and launch the product with the help of a crowdfunding platform, then go to production in the Far-East. The story is real, there is no need for artificial, sugar coated marketing video.

The campaign starts. Success. After only 5 days the project is already funded, still having almost a month left. The team is happy and it is time to look for a manufacturer. With the help of a consulting firm they find a big Asian company, finding the business promising. LOI (Letter Of Intent) signed, NDA (Non-Disclosure Agreement) signed, plans sent. After some alignment calls the team signs the contract and pays the first one-time costs. The customer is super positive and says YES to everything. Big relief for the team, isn't it? It would have been better if the startup studied some of the intercultural differences before blindly accepting all they read or hear from the supplier. Yes is not always equal to "yes, we are able to do that with all the information provided". In some countries it is, while in some others it just expresses the wish to cooperate, but further discussions are needed. False assumptions occurring from cultural misunderstandings can be expensive.

> At this point, it would be interesting to see the business plan and know the conditions the contract manufacturer gave in their offer and the terms that were signed in the contract.

The team has a missing competency: they do not have any experience with NPI (New Product Implementation) and the project management related to it. No issue, the promised delivery to backers is still feasible.

However, during the preparation for mass production some complications arise. A new sewing machine needs to be bought, because the chosen material is too robust, and the supplier wants the startup to pay for it. This is an unplanned investment. If they pay for it, there is no lunch for the team from the next day on. They decide on changing the material, which is softer, but will not last as long as the original one. They are afraid of compliance issues, but they put those fears aside, as this is the only way to survive.

4 weeks are lost making this decision. The time plan is no longer realistic and the first worried backers are starting to send inquiries about the product. The team focuses on solving issues, so there is no time for dealing with worrying customers. Anyway, it is not clear who should reply to them.

Time flies and mass production still has not started. Ramp-up production is about to start, when PANDEMIC hits, right at the area where the manufacturer is located. The whole region is blocked and after three months of lockdown the manufacturer goes bankrupt. The team stays calm and looks for another manufacturer, but by this time they have lost almost all of their money. There is no hope, none of the potential partners are interested, since they do not want to take the financial risk.

This is the sad story of a good product.

Lessons learned:

- You need to make your roadmap first and always have a clear plan.
- You need to learn how the industry you would like to work with or step into works.
- Prototyping technologies are not necessarily bad, but the mass production technologies can be a whole lot different in sense of quality, cost, and production necessities. The investment cost of a plastic injection tool alone, and the necessity of the mature design makes it harder to make major changes in design or technologies used afterwards.
- You need to understand the cultural differences, even between neighboring countries.
- Quality and product compliance are probably the most important parts of a physical product.
- Transparent communication towards customers is critical, even if you have problems. Have the roles clearly set in your team regarding who should deal with those tasks.

#3·3·6 Case 2 – Smart kitchen gadget, big plan, and market(?)

A complete NPI project team of a big company producing small kitchen appliances sits together at the end of the year. All of them are tired, but positive. A good conversation starts on how they could step on the next level. What if they establish a small engineering office and build their own product? Good idea, isn't it?

A top team for a HW startup – **or at least they believe it is** – starts to brainstorm on a product. All of them love English breakfast, so the winning idea is to make a smart English-breakfast-cooker, which enables you to order the machine to make your breakfast in advance, for every morning. It sends you a message, when the meal is ready or when something is missing.

The design is made after work and at the weekends, but in only three months time there is a prototype-ready plan and a detailed specification on the table. Time to look for a manufacturer!

If you have a certain level of awareness, you can already see that there is no person responsible for the business development, who could start the real validation process.

They start the RFQ (Request For Quotations) phase and the potential partners are happy, as the package they received is rich in information. One potential contract manufacturer is interested. NDA signed, LOI signed. Planning of the production starts.

Soon they receive a quote of a semi-automated production line in a value of 2M EUR. Moment of SHOCK.

Since the team worked for a big company, where the budget was not fixed and everything was 'for free' due to in-house production, they were not aware of the costs such a great investment can incur. The manufacturer offers to invest this money in the startup, but they ask for equity and a proof of product-market fit. The CEO of the startup reassures the manufacturing company that the product idea is great and soon they will start a crowdfunding campaign with a target of 500K EUR; and with this traction they will go for a 4M EUR investment.

The team hired a professional agency to make the Kickstarter campaign, which technically is more than perfect. Still, the campaign fails. No interest from the backers, not even 20% of the goal is reached.

Sad end for the startup.

Lessons learned:

- Validation, validation, validation. It is a waste of time, money and effort to bring a product to the market without knowing how it will perform. Of course, there is no exact tool to give you a 100% accurate number, but it can show whether the product solves real problems with customers ready to pay for it, or not.
- The innovation/change-adaptation curve teaches you an important lesson. You can plan an innovative product to be sold in high numbers, but the early adopters may

not wish for the same as the late majority. If you make a product for the second one, you need to have a cheap product with a mature design and without any issues, owning countless positive reviews. Choose your target group wisely!

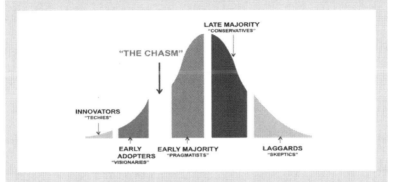

- The production model is part of the business model, and its investment costs are part of the financial plan. If you do not consider these points, you will have some sad insights later.

#3·3·7 Case 3 — White label product and a team of juniors

There are two founders of a medtech startup, having some corporate background. After making the first prototype, investors are standing in line. Funding granted, first employees boarding. A pack of young graduates need to start in-house production with FDA-compatible quality without owning enough senior experience.

It is a lucky situation, when the founders are experienced seniors with a good idea, and there is even a need on the market for the solution they offer. This is where this startup starts its journey. The founders are highly experienced engineers. They build the first prototype and start the pitches. Instant success.

Capital is no problem, and since they know how much such a development costs, they manage to collect enough money to start. The team grows with young and motivated engineers. The business grows as well and the founders have to take care of more and more business related topics, since the technological platform they build may be used by many big companies and hospitals. On the business side, selling to big companies takes time and effort. The two CEOs learn this the hard way. Different requirements in quality, design and logistics make the team replan over and over again. At the same time, the development progress does not run as expected: without the founders on site, the team of juniors need to reinvent the wheel themselves, there is some senior experience missing.

> A good idea could be to involve a larger, more experienced company or an engineering office for co-development.

Slowly, the final product reaches maturity and production can be planned. The team decides on in-house production, but how? The knowledge on how to plan and build assembly lines, how to design the process, material flow, the size of the warehouse and the related financial consequences are all missing. This means a six-months delay again, adding up to the detours in the development process.

There are some special certifications necessary to be able to ship the products, as the new quality manager has said. And he was right. Unexpected costs and delay again.

The product finally reaches the market – after more than a year of delay, compared to the initial timing plan agreed with the customers. No time to relax, there are plenty of issues to solve. The team is happy, but exhausted. Some seniors will board soon to support production, and elevate the business to the next level.

Lessons learned:

- Cost of knowledge is high. If you do not pay it upfront, you will pay more afterwards. 20 years of engineering experience in the right field are by far not equal to 20 highly motivated juniors with practically no experience.
- B2B sales have a long decision cycle time. Prepare, plan and involve professionals of that specific field you would like to enter.
- Specification of the product is made considering the following: validated customer needs, quality and production requirements, legal requirements, and compliance.
- Choosing the fitting production model can be a critical decision
- The job of the startup does not end at the start of delivery. There are new challenges occurring from keeping up delivery, scaling sales, and dealing with customer claims.

#4 Lean startup

With a background as a mechanical engineer and experience gained at production companies, I have quickly learned the importance of processes. If you think about startups, good processes are not among the top characteristics coming to your mind.

In 2011 one of my favorite publishers, Penguin Random House released a book with a title, The Lean Startup by Eric Ries, which changed my way of thinking about startups completely. Eric Ries gave us a framework based on widely used automotive quality tools and transformed them into a method easily understood by people outside the automotive industry as well. This book has shown me that no venture on earth needs frameworks and processes more than startups, since they do not have the size and inertia of a big company, but need to survive with limited opportunities and extremely scarce resources. If they make a mistake, there is a big chance their game is over – at least for that round.

As have we mentioned in the previous chapter, we resonate with the principles of the lean startup method. It provides a clear system based on verified tools originating from the Japanese automotive industry (Toyota) and a philosophy to minimize or eliminate all the waste during production, to improve ourselves and the processes and to be humble and systematic, with a purpose of giving customers nothing but the highest quality. This is what we call lean manufacturing nowadays. Lean, since you remove all the unnecessary parts, just like those of the meat bought from the butcher, to get the essence of it.

First of all, we would like to highlight some of the key principles of the original lean philosophy of the Toyota production system, which may also provide a massive base for startups to succeed:

- **Learn at the Gemba, Do at the Gemba, Teach at the Gemba.**
- Gemba is the place where the value is produced, which could be a shop floor, a production line or machines at production companies. You need to go there to understand the problem on the spot to be able to find the best solution for it.
- **Go and see for yourself to thoroughly understand the situation! (Genchi Genbutsu)**
- **Make decisions slowly, by consensus, thoroughly considering all options; implement decisions rapidly! (Nemawashi)**
- This point may seem contradictory to the scenario we observe in the lean startup method and validated learning, but it is not. You will see!
- **Standardized tasks and processes are the base for continuous improvement and employee empowerment.** 5S is a helpful tool in that:
  - Sort: Sort out unneeded items
  - Straighten: Have a place for everything
  - Shine: Keep the area clean
  - Standardize: Create rules and standard operating procedures
  - Sustain: Maintain the system and continue to improve it
- **Become a learning organization through relentless reflection (hansei) and continuous improvement (kaizen)!**

More on those principles in the book *The Toyota Way: 14 Management Principles from the World's Greatest Manufacturer* by Jeffrey Liker. We highly recommend reading it and also consulting experts working with this framework to be able to understand the higher idea behind it completely.

This is an ideology that could be difficult to adapt if you are not working in the automotive or other manufacturing industries, but Eric Ries saw the opportunity and turned these principles into an adaptation for the startup scene. In this chapter we will give you an overview of the method, list the tools and introduce the use and limitations of it.

As you will see, the main limitation here is the user and not the tool, since being easy to understand does not mean that all startups using the methods described in the book will make any startup lean. The lean startup method has proved to be one of the best frameworks so far, making the fall at least softer, but not in every case avoidable, and if you have also failed before, you may have realized that it was not the framework's fault. It is more, how it was or was not applied. To be successful, it needs to be digested, fine-tuned and integrated into the daily life of a future unicorn. As a first step let's get familiar with the framework, or get a refresher on it!

#4·1 The essence of the Lean Startup

You would like to build something fantastic, but your resources are more than limited. The resource can be money, time, knowledge (or more experience) or anything else critical for your project, but for most startuppers trying to make their dreams come true after their full-time jobs and out of their savings, these resources are not available in endless amounts. You – as the one-person-team of the project, or the leader or member of a handful of dedicated innovators – need to work with what you have and try to make the best out of it, which often feels like balancing on a very thin rope while solving high level mathematical problems.

Eric Ries depicted this situation in a really expressive analogy: jumping off a cliff and trying to build an airplane while falling. Does not sound easy or stress-free, does it?

The most important part of building a lean startup is to be aware of the situation, to continuously monitor the current scenario and future possibilities, adapt and improve to be able to survive. In quality assurance, the foundation of the Continuous Improvement Process (CIP) is the PDCA cycle. First of all, you **PLAN** what, why and how you are going to do. Then you **DO** it. After it is done, you **CHECK** the results and compare them to the expected outcome. In case the outcome is not what you expected, you will need some corrective **ACT**ions.

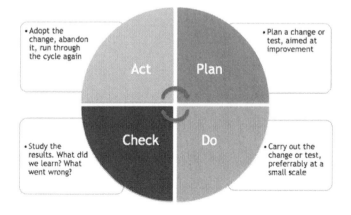

- Adopt the change, abandon it, run through the cycle again

Act

- Plan a change or test, aimed at improvement

Plan

Check

- Study the results. What did we learn? What went wrong?

Do

- Carry out the change or test, preferably at a small scale

The B-M-L cycle introduced by Eric Ries is practically the PDCA cycle applied in the startup environment. In this circular model let's start off with you as a startupper, who would like to acquire the essential knowledge that makes you successful. To get this information, you **BUILD** a minimalistic, simplified test model, which is going to be the minimum viable product (MVP). You would like to test whether the hypotheses in your mind are correct, so after you have built your prototype, your dummy, or whatever serves you the best, you go to the market and **MEASURE** how it works in real life. During this whole process you are going to **LEARN** a lot, especially if you repeat the cycle multiple times, which helps you on your way – if you are lean enough.

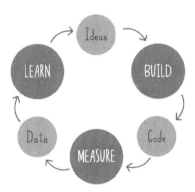

Let's see an example of the learning process! Your top priority is to validate your idea. You build a landing page for your product targeting your future customers.

What kind of information can you gain, what can you learn?

- How your target audience responds to your value proposition
- How valuable (in a measurable way) the interaction is

- How the decision making process of your customers is built up
- etc.

This information package is the critical core, the foundation for your startup. The more you understand about what happens outside your head, the more your biased assumptions are destroyed and the more likely you will find the real needs of your customers. There are several tools in the lean startup toolbox to help you understand your customers and their pain.

The ultimate tool is the MVP: Minimum Viable Product. MVP means something already good enough to help you learn by becoming a tool for validation. It is something the customers can already see, use and evaluate, providing you information on whether you offer the right solution to the right problem. This can be anything: a mockup, a prototype (with limited or selected features), a landing page, or anything that works and enables you to test how the customers react to your offer and measure the results. Briefly, MVP enables you to validate and decide whether to pivot or stay on the same track in the future.

Besides building an MVP, there are numerous learning tools from AB testing to customer interviews, which can help you in gathering information, if you use them well. Learning is a process, not a one-time occasion: any of the tools, which you use, you need to repeat the cycle multiple times to gain real results. Use a tool, measure the result, process it and adopt the new knowledge. This is a B-M-L cycle as well. There is one main goal that the B-M-L cycle and the MVP serve: validated learning.

You need to learn as fast as possible and on the smallest possible budget. This, hopefully, gives you enough opportunities for direction-adjustments instead of heading towards a completely wrong direction. Let's call these direction-adjustments pivots or persevere points – the points where the team decides whether to keep the direction or change it – sometimes drastically – based on what they have learned from the customers.

This is why this method is lean. You try to get rid of the unnecessary detours, processes and parts of the tasks. You constantly strive to make the most progress and at least possible cost (in time, money and other resources) and the goal is to progress and not not to spend.

#4·2 Tools and usage of the lean method

Lean startup and its application has been diluted a little bit. Instead of focusing on how it changes the process and how aggressively you have to go through cycles, most outlets focus on how it changes your thinking. This is of course also important, and useful to some extent but can easily become counterproductive if you only focus on the thinking process and avoid changing the execution itself. Our experience is that not only the execution process is often excluded from transformation, but also the way lean startup focus should change your way of thinking about a problem.

Let's take a look at how the lean startup method should change your way of thinking about a problem and the tools of changing the process.

1. Solve the right problem – and do it the right way
   Extremely strong customer focus; and agile, aggressive hypothesis-building and validation are the two key aspects of the agile framework that lean startups apply.
   However, customer focus usually stops at 'how do I get my next 5-10-50 clients?'. If you focus on the real problem of people instead of focusing on getting the clients at first, the solution is going to bring the customers too. So listen to them and validate before trying to sell them a solution they do not need! With this on your dashboard, some decisions may completely change.

2. Think long term
   Operating on the B2B market or doing a hardware startup, you will also have to ask yourself: will the solution work on a global scale? Can it serve ten thousand users the same way it does ten only? This applies to both technical and business decisions, since you may opt for cheaper or less time-enduring solutions to speed up the spread and save money, but bear in mind that sooner or later it will always fall back on you.

3. Understand the problem and the process
   In the lean startup methodology it was never expected to reinvent the wheel. You should rather understand why the wheel was actually invented in that form and what the problem was, for which the wheel came as an answer. If you understand the problem and the process, you will be able to innovate and not just make another solution, which might be slightly better than the previous one.

4. Execute lean, not cheap

   Here we have to clear some of the misconceptions about what being lean is about: lean methodology means spending as little as you can to validate hypotheses as quickly as possible, but it does not mean building the best solution from the smallest possible amount of money. On the other hand, lean also means figuring out whether you should make the next step or not, and finding the right direction to move forward before spending on it. To sum it up, it is a set of distinct points you are trying to connect throughout your journey. It is figuring out what is the next best step to get to the absolute top.

5. Skip small, plan big from the beginning

   You need to focus on all the factors and run the Build-Measure-Learn cycles simultaneously on many levels from the very beginning. You need to have the helicopter view all the time and see the big picture also while fighting your small battles. This is like a war, where you are the general, the lieutenant, the major and the private at the same time.

6. Do not take things for granted

   Everything is a hypothesis. This is probably the most challenging part of all. It is extremely difficult to realize the things you are taking for granted, whereas it might very well be just an assumption. So at every step of the journey, you need to ask yourself: is this valid information or just a hypothesis? The only reliable answer is the one coming from the market, from your future customers. Understanding it right is another story.

#4·3 Limitations of the lean methodology

Even though the lean startup method is really useful, it carries numerous risks as well. It is easy to cheat yourself into the belief that your startup is running lean, which is even more critical in case of hardware products. You can easily believe that you are doing things right, even if you are just randomly using the tools. Rapid changes may fool you in the beginning, but maintaining development and integrating into your culture is the real use we are looking for. Complexity itself puts tremendous pressure on you. Staying lean, meanwhile getting answers rich in information enough not to distort any part of the complex system is definitely not an easy task. For this extra challenge, the basic framework calls for an update and higher awareness of this complexity.

There is another important point, where we need to form our critique. It is not trivial, how the method handles situations, when the objectives and the knowledge are continuously refined. With every step of validation you might receive information that could totally rearrange the mental map of the project. These details may also support or disprove the hypothesis you wanted to validate. Which information bit should be used, and how, this is what no tool of the method answers you clearly enough.

The internal mini-projects are also not really considered, meanwhile they are an important part of the daily struggles of the startups. You need to build not only the product, but also the company around it with all the processes, starting with knowledge processing and organizing, which are the backbone of the validation and later the development. Agile and Scrum methods – the current fastest developing and widely-used frameworks –

may help you here, but they are not the holy grail either and using them properly is not an easy job.

We will discover in the upcoming chapter, how the current framework can be developed and which further tools can be used.

#5 Updated framework

As we saw in chapter #3, startups tend to fail, even if all the team members do their best. The biggest mistake they usually make is forgetting to stay disciplined, whatever happens. Many teams get in a party mood easily after every little success, but are also quickly depressed by the downs. This journey is really like a spacewalk. You need to stay alert, focused and sometimes refocus, if necessary. There is no room to lose time or waste resources. This is why we would like to provide these teams with updated tools, handrails and safety helmets from time to time, to ensure we give our best to support them, or catch them in time if they fall.

A framework is good if it helps the project in planning, execution, and control by providing us with methods and forming our mindset. This may sound easy, but as for the HW startups, the depth and the complexity makes the game more difficult than it might seem at first.

A good framework is rich in tools, processes and best practices to be able to support you in any situation from the beginning of your journey to the very end. The building blocks of it should originate from the most developed industries and/or the current best frameworks. For a long period of time, the tools of the automotive industry have been the most efficient, refining the basic principles of quality assurance processes and ensuring repeatable high quality. As we have discussed before, these tools were applied in the lean startup framework for the rapid scaling of ideas to companies, widely used by startups. As you will see, we have also kept the track bound to the automotive quality tools and picked and added some more of them to extend the original functionality.

A good framework should also remain flexible and contain enough tools to enable the user to cherrypick the right ones for a particular case. The main goal of our updates is to collect the right tools to build a system that regenerates the mindset from time to time and directs your focus where it needs to be. Every journey is different and so are the processes of planning and the tools necessary. Here, we aim to show you a toolbox, not a 'one-fits-all' package. Out of the pieces at hand, you need to construct a method yourself that fits your purpose; a system that brings clarity, discipline, and predictability and turns the red lamps on soon enough to be able to take action. Use all the building blocks the way it suits you best, but never forget to be consistent and transparent towards your team and partners!

The tool updates and additional tools we offer you can be separated into three groups, which build a global B-M-L cycle, as follows:

- Execution tools → Build,
- Alignment and control tools → Measure,
- Learning tools → Learn,

These, we are going to discuss not in this order, but as learning, execution, and control tool packages.

#5·1 Learning tools

There is no activity more important in the life of the startups than processing information and using the knowledge to improve and this is the reason why we are going to introduce **learning tools in the first group**. The tools discussed below are based on the lean methodology and the current best practices in project management, which may already be a great help as they are, however, we have made some adjustments to make them easier to use and more valuable for HW startups.

In chapter #3, where we have already shared our thoughts on why hardware startups are way more complex than others, which means that the basic B-M-L cycle needs to be elaborated to be able to handle this level of complexity. We have called the modified model the [Build-Measure-Learn-Adapt]^X cycle, as you need to integrate the learning cycle into four main domains, Business, Technology, People, Finances, which we are going to introduce in Chapters #6 and #7 more in details.

At the first step of the model – just like in the BML cycle – you **build** a dummy, working model, prototype or anything else containing the essence of your idea, with the purpose of learning. Your goal with this step may be learning about

- customers
- the way customers use the product
- thoughts of customers on the product
- business model
- pricing strategy
- marketing

- materials used
- long-time behavior of the product
- new features

Eric Ries has already introduced several forms of the MVP, which work well for many (SW) startups, but unfortunately, at HW products you are going to have much more to test and learn than. However, in the meantime, MVP has developed as well and turned into **Minimum X Y**, where you can substitute **X** with:

- Viable,
- Lovable,
- Marketable,
- Sellable,
- Remarkable,
- etc.,

and **Y** with:

- Product,
- Service,
- Experience

Minimum X Y
What should you build?

This model is an integration of many great thoughts and summarizes the essence of the hard job: finding the best tool to get the best result. The reason for adding this to our framework is simple: the validation phase here is more critical than ever. You can easily invest millions of dollars or euros into the mass production of your product idea, only to face the fact at the market launch that there is no real customer need for it or people have no idea how to use it. Most of us know at least one product, for which the team has missed the lecture of validated learning.

To give you some handrails, we are going to introduce some of the MXYs, however, you can create unique ones, if you need. The main goal is to measure what matters, right? Keeping the game lean, first you need to find the parts of the product you need to test. Since you cannot read the mind of your (future) customers, you need to be as specific as possible: highlight what you need to test and blur what is not important.

Choosing the right MXY again and again gives you the backlog of the product development, which you need to turn into specification later. The development process at HW startups differs from the SW development. You need to test different MXYs together, or parallel at HW, while at SW products you can get by with a series of one-by-one testings of MXYs relying on each other linearly.

One of the most interesting MXY is the MVX, often also called MVE: the Minimum Valuable Experience. At HW startups experience is not scaled the same way as at SW, you need to develop something very similar to the endproduct for the first time, there are no possibilities for continuous add-ons, as the image below shows:

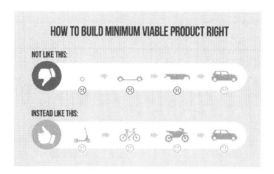

If your product is a car, your MXY cannot be a seat, wheel or a dashboard alone, it should solve the same problem, from the first prototype on, maybe less good materials, less nice design, not the final SW, and not the final business model.

When it comes to testing, the most important thing is to know what you actually would like to **measure** or find out and to have an assumption or hypothesis you would like to test, which is measurable in a quantitative or qualitative way. Without clear assumptions all you are going to have is a massive amount of information without any practical use.

After you have collected the results, you need to understand their meaning and conclude the lessons to be **learnt**. The interpretation of these results can be crucial, but if you have made clear and measurable assumptions, the only thing you need to figure out is how you can use the information for your own good. Henry Ford had a well-quoted sentence on that: 'If I had asked people what they wanted, they would have said faster horses.'. You need to understand what is behind 'faster horses'.

Let us assume you have understood the outcome of your experiment correctly. The next step is **adaptation**. Here, you need to evaluate the results. Seeing the outcomes, what are the changes to be made and what are the risks of them? Are they feasible? You need to evaluate the (investment) cost and the ROI of any possible changes and the way they may alter the whole roadmap, timing and plan.

At HW startups the hardware and the connecting technologies need to make you even more thoughtful. In classical product development (learnt in the automotive industry) there is a holy seance, called feasibility study. You can give your customers a 3D-printed prototype, which they may love, but if you are not able to produce it with injection molding, you are at a dead end. Therefore, you need to be very careful about how you get the desired validation and how it affects your technological stack.

After you have figured all of that out and made the decisions based on what you have learnt, there comes the next 'semester' with all new subjects and lessons to learn. To *really* learn the lessons, you need to have all the lessons documented in some form, a list of hypotheses, which, after validation, should be turned into a feature list, that can be converted into technical specification, which is going to be the backbone of the development plan. You always need to find the right questions, problems, and user behavior to validate, which is not an easy task at all. Take your time and make a proper list of hypotheses, get out of the building and test them on the battlefield one by one.

For this you do not need anything more than (Excel) sheet or a whiteboard. In this case the method is the same as for SW projects, it is only the awareness that needs to be extended on the HW. Simple as it seems, still, without this step all the hypotheses, testing and lessons are in vain.

#5·2 Execution tools

The second group are the execution tools, where we would like to quote the current (2021) Agile Manifesto, and Scrum Guide directly, without changing any word of it. We will, however, give some ideas and remarks to make it easier to digest, help understand misleading phrases and give you some thoughts on how this could serve a HW startup.

First the Agile Manifesto and its twelve principles:

We are uncovering better ways of developing
software by doing it and helping others do it.
Through this work we have come to value:

Individuals and interactions over processes and tools
Working software over comprehensive documentation
Customer collaboration over contract negotiation
Responding to change over following a plan

That is, while there is value in the items on
the right, we value the items on the left more.

1. *Our highest priority is to satisfy the customer through early and continuous delivery of valuable software.*

2. Welcome changing requirements, even late in development. Agile processes harness change for the customer's competitive advantage.
3. Deliver working software frequently, from a couple of weeks to a couple of months, with a preference to the shorter timescale.
4. Business people and developers must work together daily throughout the project.
5. Build projects around motivated individuals. Give them the environment and support they need, and trust them to get the job done.
6. The most efficient and effective method of conveying information to and within a development team is face-to-face conversation.
7. Working software is the primary measure of progress.
8. Agile processes promote sustainable development. The sponsors, developers, and users should be able to maintain a constant pace indefinitely.
9. Continuous attention to technical excellence and good design enhances agility.
10. Simplicity – the art of maximizing the amount of work not done – is essential.
11. The best architectures, requirements, and designs emerge from self-organizing teams.
12. At regular intervals, the team reflects on how to become more effective, then tunes and adjusts its behavior accordingly.

After the first reading, you can hardly ever think that this manifesto and principles can help HW startups; especially when keeping the importance of discipline, planning, and documentation in mind. Yes, you are right, partially. To see how it could still help you, you need to understand the philosophy behind it. Let us introduce the Scrum Guide, which brings some more interesting views to the table. Together they can help you understand why SW development evolved to the point where it is now.

Scrum Definition

Scrum is a lightweight framework that helps people, teams and organizations generate value through adaptive solutions for complex problems.

In a nutshell, Scrum requires a Scrum Master to foster an environment where:

- *A Product Owner orders the work for a complex problem into a Product Backlog.*
- *The Scrum Team turns a selection of the work into an Increment of value during a Sprint.*
- *The Scrum Team and its stakeholders inspect the results and adjust for the next Sprint.*
- *Repeat*

Scrum is simple. Try it as is and determine if its philosophy, theory, and structure help to achieve goals and create value. The Scrum framework is purposefully incomplete, only defining the parts required to implement Scrum theory. Scrum is built upon by the collective intelligence of the people using it. Rather than provide people with detailed instructions, the rules of Scrum guide their relationships and interactions.

Various processes, techniques and methods can be employed within the framework. Scrum wraps around existing practices or renders them unnecessary. Scrum makes visible the relative efficacy of current management, environment, and work techniques, so that improvements can be made.

Scrum Theory

Scrum is founded on empiricism and lean thinking. Empiricism asserts that knowledge comes from experience and making decisions based on what is observed. Lean thinking reduces waste and focuses on the essentials.

Scrum employs an iterative, incremental approach to optimize predictability and to control risk. Scrum engages groups of people who collectively have all the skills and expertise to do the work and share or acquire such skills as needed.

Scrum combines four formal events for inspection and adaptation within a containing event, the Sprint. These events work because they implement the empirical Scrum pillars of transparency, inspection, and adaptation.

Transparency

The emergent process and work must be visible to those performing the work as well as those receiving the work. With Scrum, important decisions are based on the perceived state of its three formal artifacts. Artifacts that have low transparency can lead to decisions that diminish value and increase risk.

Transparency enables inspection. Inspection without transparency is misleading and wasteful.

Inspection

The Scrum artifacts and the progress toward agreed goals must be inspected frequently and diligently to detect potentially undesirable variances or problems. To help with inspection, Scrum provides cadence in the form of its five events.

Inspection enables adaptation. Inspection without adaptation is considered pointless. Scrum events are designed to provoke change.

Adaptation

If any aspects of a process deviate outside acceptable limits or if the resulting product is unacceptable, the process being applied or the materials being produced must be adjusted. The adjustment must be made as soon as possible to minimize further deviation.

Adaptation becomes more difficult when the people involved are not empowered or self-managing. A Scrum Team is expected to adapt the moment it learns anything new through inspection.

Scrum Values

Successful use of Scrum depends on people becoming more proficient in living five values:

Commitment, Focus, Openness, Respect, and Courage

The Scrum Team commits to achieving its goals and to

supporting each other. Their primary focus is on the work of the Sprint to make the best possible progress toward these goals. The Scrum Team and its stakeholders are open about the work and the challenges. Scrum Team members respect each other to be capable, independent people, and are respected as such by the people with whom they work. The Scrum Team members have the courage to do the right thing, to work on tough problems.

These values give direction to the Scrum Team with regard to their work, actions, and behavior. The decisions that are made, the steps taken, and the way Scrum is used should reinforce these values, not diminish or undermine them. The Scrum Team members learn and explore the values as they work with the Scrum events and artifacts. When these values are embodied by the Scrum Team and the people they work with, the empirical Scrum pillars of transparency, inspection, and adaptation come to life building trust.

Scrum Team

The fundamental unit of Scrum is a small team of people, a Scrum Team. The Scrum Team consists of one Scrum Master, one Product Owner, and Developers. Within a Scrum Team, there are no sub-teams or hierarchies. It is a cohesive unit of professionals focused on one objective at a time, the Product Goal.

Scrum Teams are cross-functional, meaning the members have all the skills necessary to create value each Sprint. They are also self-managing, meaning they internally decide who does what, when, and how.

The Scrum Team is small enough to remain nimble and large enough to complete significant work within a Sprint, typically 10 or fewer people. In general, we have found that smaller teams communicate better and are more productive. If Scrum Teams become too large, they should consider reorganizing into multiple cohesive Scrum Teams, each focused on the same product. Therefore, they should share the same Product Goal, Product Backlog, and Product Owner.

The Scrum Team is responsible for all product-related activities from stakeholder collaboration, verification, maintenance, operation, experimentation, research and development, and anything else that might be required. They are structured and empowered by the organization to manage their own work. Working in Sprints at a sustainable pace improves the Scrum Team's focus and consistency.

The entire Scrum Team is accountable for creating a valuable, useful Increment every Sprint. Scrum defines three specific accountabilities within the Scrum Team: the Developers, the Product Owner, and the Scrum Master.

Developers

Developers are the people in the Scrum Team that are committed to creating any aspect of a usable Increment each Sprint.

The specific skills needed by the Developers are often broad and will vary with the domain of work. However, the Developers are always accountable for:

- Creating a plan for the Sprint, the Sprint Backlog;
- Instilling quality by adhering to a Definition of Done;
- Adapting their plan each day toward the Sprint Goal; and,
- Holding each other accountable as professionals.

Product Owner

The Product Owner is accountable for maximizing the value of the product resulting from the work of the Scrum Team. How this is done may vary widely across organizations, Scrum Teams, and individuals.

The Product Owner is also accountable for effective Product Backlog management, which includes:

- Developing and explicitly communicating the Product Goal;
- Creating and clearly communicating Product Backlog items;
- Ordering Product Backlog items; and,
- Ensuring that the Product Backlog is transparent, visible and understood.

The Product Owner may do the above work or may delegate the responsibility to others. Regardless, the Product Owner remains accountable.

For Product Owners to succeed, the entire organization must respect their decisions. These decisions are visible in the content and ordering of the Product Backlog, and through the inspectable Increment at the Sprint Review.

The Product Owner is one person, not a committee. The Product Owner may represent the needs of many stake-holders in the Product Backlog. Those wanting to change the Product Backlog can do so by trying to convince the Product Owner.

Scrum Master

The Scrum Master is accountable for establishing Scrum as defined in the Scrum Guide. They do this by helping every-one understand Scrum theory and practice, both within the Scrum Team and the organization.

The Scrum Master is accountable for the Scrum Team's ef-fectiveness. They do this by enabling the Scrum Team to improve its practices, within the Scrum framework.

Scrum Masters are true leaders who serve the Scrum Team and the larger organization.

The Scrum Master serves the Scrum Team in several ways, including:

- Coaching the team members in self-management and cross-functionality;
- Helping the Scrum Team focus on creating high-value In-crements that meet the Definition of Done;
- Causing the removal of impediments to the Scrum Team's progress; and,
- Ensuring that all Scrum events take place and are posi-tive, productive, and kept within the timebox.

The Scrum Master serves the Product Owner in several ways, including:

- Helping find techniques for effective Product Goal definition and Product Backlog management;
- Helping the Scrum Team understand the need for clear and concise Product Backlog items;
- Helping establish empirical product planning for a complex environment; and,
- Facilitating stakeholder collaboration as requested or needed.

The Scrum Master serves the organization in several ways, including:

- Leading, training, and coaching the organization in its Scrum adoption;
- Planning and advising Scrum implementations within the organization;
- Helping employees and stakeholders understand and enact an empirical approach for complex work; and,
- Removing barriers between stakeholders and Scrum Teams.

Scrum Events

The Sprint is a container for all other events. Each event in Scrum is a formal opportunity to inspect and adapt Scrum artifacts. These events are specifically designed to enable the transparency required. Failure to operate any events as prescribed results in lost opportunities to inspect and adapt. Events are used in Scrum to create regularity and to minimize the need for meetings not defined in Scrum.

Optimally, all events are held at the same time and place to reduce complexity.

The Sprint

Sprints are the heartbeat of Scrum, where ideas are turned into value.

They are fixed length events of one month or less to create consistency. A new Sprint starts immediately after the conclusion of the previous Sprint.

All the work necessary to achieve the Product Goal, including Sprint Planning, Daily Scrums, Sprint Review, and Sprint Retrospective, happen within Sprints.

During the Sprint:

- No changes are made that would endanger the Sprint Goal;
- Quality does not decrease;
- The Product Backlog is refined as needed; and,
- Scope may be clarified and renegotiated with the Product Owner as more is learned.

Sprints enable predictability by ensuring inspection and adaptation of progress toward a Product Goal at least every calendar month. When a Sprint's horizon is too long the Sprint Goal may become invalid, complexity may rise, and risk may increase. Shorter Sprints can be employed to generate more learning cycles and limit risk of cost and effort to a smaller time frame. Each Sprint may be considered a short project.

Various practices exist to forecast progress, like burn-downs, burn-ups, or cumulative flows. While proven useful, these do not replace the importance of empiricism. In complex environments, what will happen is unknown. Only what has already happened may be used for forward-looking decision making.

A Sprint could be cancelled if the Sprint Goal becomes obsolete. Only the Product Owner has the authority to cancel the Sprint.

Sprint Planning

Sprint Planning initiates the Sprint by laying out the work to be performed for the Sprint. This resulting plan is created by the collaborative work of the entire Scrum Team.

The Product Owner ensures that attendees are prepared to discuss the most important Product Backlog items and how they map to the Product Goal. The Scrum Team may also invite other people to attend Sprint Planning to provide advice.

Sprint Planning addresses the following topics:

Topic One: Why is this Sprint valuable?
The Product Owner proposes how the product could increase its value and utility in the current Sprint. The whole Scrum Team then collaborates to define a Sprint Goal that communicates why the Sprint is valuable to stakeholders. The Sprint Goal must be finalized prior to the end of Sprint Planning.

Topic Two: What can be Done this Sprint?

Through discussion with the Product Owner, the Developers select items from the Product Backlog to include in the current Sprint. The Scrum Team may refine these items during this process, which increases understanding and confidence.

Selecting how much can be completed within a Sprint may be challenging. However, the more the Developers know about their past performance, their upcoming capacity, and their Definition of Done, the more confident they will be in their Sprint forecasts.

Topic Three: How will the chosen work get done?

For each selected Product Backlog item, the Developers plan the work necessary to create an Increment that meets the Definition of Done. This is often done by decomposing Product Backlog items into smaller work items of one day or less. How this is done is at the sole discretion of the Developers. No one else tells them how to turn Product Backlog items into Increments of value.

The Sprint Goal, the Product Backlog items selected for the Sprint, plus the plan for delivering them are together referred to as the Sprint Backlog.

Sprint Planning is timeboxed to a maximum of eight hours for a one-month Sprint. For shorter Sprints, the event is usually shorter.

Daily Scrum

The purpose of the Daily Scrum is to inspect progress toward the Sprint Goal and adapt the Sprint Backlog as necessary, adjusting the upcoming planned work.

The Daily Scrum is a 15-minute event for the Developers of the Scrum Team. To reduce complexity, it is held at the same time and place every working day of the Sprint. If the Product Owner or Scrum Master are actively working on items in the Sprint Backlog, they participate as Developers.

The Developers can select whatever structure and techniques they want, as long as their Daily Scrum focuses on progress toward the Sprint Goal and produces an actionable plan for the next day of work. This creates focus and improves self-management.

Daily Scrums improve communications, identify impediments, promote quick decision-making, and consequently eliminate the need for other meetings.

The Daily Scrum is not the only time Developers are allowed to adjust their plan. They often meet throughout the day for more detailed discussions about adapting or re-planning the rest of the Sprint's work.

Sprint Review

The purpose of the Sprint Review is to inspect the outcome of the Sprint and determine future adaptations. The Scrum Team presents the results of their work to key stakeholders and progress toward the Product Goal is discussed.

During the event, the Scrum Team and stakeholders re-view what was accomplished in the Sprint and what has changed in their environment. Based on this information, attendees collaborate on what to do next. The Product Backlog may also be adjusted to meet new opportunities. The Sprint Review is a working session and the Scrum Team should avoid limiting it to a presentation.

The Sprint Review is the second to last event of the Sprint and is timeboxed to a maximum of four hours for a one-month Sprint. For shorter Sprints, the event is usually shorter.

Sprint Retrospective

The purpose of the Sprint Retrospective is to plan ways to increase quality and effectiveness.

The Scrum Team inspects how the last Sprint went with regards to individuals, interactions, processes, tools, and their Definition of Done. Inspected elements often vary with the domain of work. Assumptions that led them astray are identified and their origins explored. The Scrum Team discusses what went well during the Sprint, what problems it encountered, and how those problems were (or were not) solved.

The Scrum Team identifies the most helpful changes to im-prove its effectiveness. The most impactful improvements are addressed as soon as possible. They may even be add-ed to the Sprint Backlog for the next Sprint.

The Sprint Retrospective concludes the Sprint. It is time-boxed to a maximum of three hours for a one-month Sprint. For shorter Sprints, the event is usually shorter.

Scrum Artifacts

Scrum's artifacts represent work or value. They are designed to maximize transparency of key information. Thus, everyone inspecting them has the same basis for adaptation.

Each artifact contains a commitment to ensure it provides information that enhances transparency and focus against which progress can be measured:

- For the Product Backlog it is the Product Goal.
- For the Sprint Backlog it is the Sprint Goal.
- For the Increment it is the Definition of Done.

These commitments exist to reinforce empiricism and the Scrum values for the Scrum Team and their stakeholders.

Product Backlog

The Product Backlog is an emergent, ordered list of what is needed to improve the product. It is the single source of work undertaken by the Scrum Team.

Product Backlog items that can be Done by the Scrum Team within one Sprint are deemed ready for selection in a Sprint Planning event. They usually acquire this degree of transparency after refining activities. Product Backlog refinement is the act of breaking down and further defining Product Backlog items into smaller more precise items. This is an ongoing activity to add details, such as a description, order, and size. Attributes often vary with the domain of work.

The Developers who will be doing the work are responsible for the sizing. The Product Owner may influence the Developers by helping them understand and select trade-offs.

Commitment: Product Goal

The Product Goal describes a future state of the product which can serve as a target for the Scrum Team to plan against. The Product Goal is in the Product Backlog. The rest of the Product Backlog emerges to define "what" will fulfill the Product Goal.

A product is a vehicle to deliver value. It has a clear boundary, known stakeholders, well-defined users or customers. A product could be a service, a physical product, or something more abstract.

The Product Goal is the long-term objective for the Scrum Team. They must fulfill (or abandon) one objective before taking on the next.

Sprint Backlog

The Sprint Backlog is composed of the Sprint Goal (why), the set of Product Backlog items selected for the Sprint (what), as well as an actionable plan for delivering the Increment (how).

The Sprint Backlog is a plan by and for the Developers. It is a highly visible, real-time picture of the work that the Developers plan to accomplish during the Sprint in order to achieve the Sprint Goal. Consequently, the Sprint Backlog is updated throughout the Sprint as more is learned. It should have enough detail that they can inspect their progress in the Daily Scrum.

Commitment: Sprint Goal

The Sprint Goal is the single objective for the Sprint. Although the Sprint Goal is a commitment by the Developers, it provides flexibility in terms of the exact work needed to achieve it. The Sprint Goal also creates coherence and focus, encouraging the Scrum Team to work together rather than on separate initiatives.

The Sprint Goal is created during the Sprint Planning event and then added to the Sprint Backlog. As the Developers work during the Sprint, they keep the Sprint Goal in mind. If the work turns out to be different than they expected, they collaborate with the Product Owner to negotiate the scope of the Sprint Backlog within the Sprint without affecting the Sprint Goal.

Increment

An Increment is a concrete stepping stone toward the Product Goal. Each Increment is additive to all prior Increments and thoroughly verified, ensuring that all Increments work together. In order to provide value, the Increment must be usable.

Multiple Increments may be created within a Sprint. The sum of the Increments is presented at the Sprint Review thus supporting empiricism. However, an Increment may be delivered to stakeholders prior to the end of the Sprint. The Sprint Review should never be considered a gate to releasing value.

Work cannot be considered part of an Increment unless it meets the Definition of Done.

Commitment: Definition of Done

The Definition of Done is a formal description of the state of the Increment when it meets the quality measures required for the product.

The moment a Product Backlog item meets the Definition of Done, an Increment is born.

The Definition of Done creates transparency by providing everyone a shared understanding of what work was completed as part of the Increment. If a Product Backlog item does not meet the Definition of Done, it cannot be released or even presented at the Sprint Review. Instead, it returns to the Product Backlog for future consideration.

If the Definition of Done for an increment is part of the standards of the organization, all Scrum Teams must follow it as a minimum. If it is not an organizational standard, the Scrum Team must create a Definition of Done appropriate for the product.

> *The Developers are required to conform to the Definition of Done. If there are multiple Scrum Teams working together on a product, they must mutually define and comply with the same Definition of Done.*

You can find the original resources on agilemanifesto.org, and scrumguides.org.

After reading the essence of both 'religions' it is important to mention again that the field, on which agile and scrum were first used was SW development, BUT it is surely not a coincidence that more and more industries are starting to adopt them, at least to a certain extent. Nowadays SW engineering is the fastest developing and most flexible ecosystem. Methodologies like Agile and Scrum can give you principles you can follow and benefit from and they both also provide you with support during the scaling phase by SAFe and Scrum of scrums, the corporate versions of them.

What Agile and Scrum can teach us among the numerous benefits are the usefulness of new roles we need to consider, when planning the team, the customer-focused mindset through building teams with high motivation to solve the customers' problem and the framework to execute all this in a volatile environment. It also teaches us how crucial it is to keep the whole mission transparent and make the team feel responsible for customer success and value.

Of course, the speed and agility of agile delivery teams and the scrum roles, events, and artifacts are not a copy-paste story, where you tell traditional engineers to be agile from tomorrow on, and the scrum master will keep the team together. The main point here is to understand why agile and scrum have happened and why this way. The main reason was the challenge of being more and more efficient without burning unnecessary resources – something that may highly contribute to the survival of HW startups too.

We do not have a 'one-size-fits-all' tool suggestion here, just some key takeaways you should consider:

- Introduce new roles and responsibilities to reach maximum efficiency, e.g. scrum master and the product owner
- Merge the two SW development frameworks with classical company processes to form your own toolbar
- Customer satisfaction is the highest priority. If the feature list and specification list have to be changed to achieve this, it is not a waste of effort to change course.
- You can deliver SW frequently, but HW is a different story
- Planning is really important. 9:1 ratio could be a good goal. Know what, how, and why you would like to do before you start burning money
- Invest in learning and development of the team
- Daily scrum, planning events, sprint closing, hot wash, and other events are great but have to be effective. There are great experts to help you

#5·3 Alignment and control tools

The third group are the alignment and control tools, the dearest for me, and the least seriously taken by many. When a project starts, first you need to be a learning team, then a learning organization – which is easier said than done. The key factors here are the administration and documentation of every single step you take, followed by continuous revisiting and regular updating of the documentation. In my opinion the most important thing on this journey is to have a clear understanding of where we are and in which direction we are going. There has to be an initial point serving as the base, a starting point we can always relate to, see the trajectory we went through and adjust, if necessary. Without the initial point there is nothing to align to – but even if there is one, you also need to find the right tools to be able to adjust and keep control.

To be able to continuously monitor your path and align, you need to strive towards two goals:

- Owning structured knowledge updated regularly, e.g. risk assessment, feasibility study, hypothesis list, financial plan, etc.
- Building a trigger system that reacts to changes, alerts you if necessary and shows you the priorities to focus on, e.g. when you need to pivot

These alone are easily said, but thinking about them, they literally cover every aspect of a project, so are not so easy to realize. Here we give you some useful tools and tips on how to step on the right path:

- Have a project book and/or project charter – a document where you lay down all the important information you have, e.g. scope, budget, timeliness, team members, milestones, known specifications. This should be a living document you update at least at every major milestone.
- Make a timeplan for the long term and a calendar for the short term plans. Long term daily tasks can be planned in a calendar too, but you lose the big picture if you would like to make it handle the whole project. Numerous project management tools can deal with longer term plans and wider scopes in the form of a Gannt diagram for example, but an Excel sheet can suffice the purpose too.
- Have an agenda and meeting minutes for meetings. The recipe to an effective meeting is to invite the right people, inform them about the agenda, give a structure to the meeting and document the conclusions and the decisions taken in the meeting minutes.
- Do risk assessment to understand current and future risks and make decisions accordingly. This is what large ventures also do to stay alive. **Flowchart → Control Plan → D- and P-FMEA** (Design- and Process Failure Mode and Effect Analysis) is a great trio to do that. In a flowchart you outline the process, then identify where the value is generated and how you can ensure its quality. You document it in a control plan describing how you will keep the process under control, then in the D- or P-FMEA you identify the points where things can go wrong and the actions that could be taken to handle the issues.
- Do feasibility studies often and design your product for manufacturing and assembly from the beginning, since planning ahead is always cheaper than changing course

after investing in machines and spending on materials and processes.

- **DFMA** stands for Design for Manufacturing and Assembly. It is an engineering methodology focusing on reducing time-to-market and total production costs by prioritizing easy manufacturing of the product parts and simplified assembly of parts into the final product already during the early design-phases of the product lifecycle.
- **Value stream planning** is defined as a lean tool that employs a flowchart documenting every step of the process and helps you find potential problems and eliminate all kinds of waste. Plan and map the value stream of the production and assembly processes constantly to avoid detours.

- Have a rock-solid change management process. This is the only way to know what has changed, why, who asked for it and who has approved it. This may seem unnecessary, when no issues occur, but can be very useful when tracking the root cause of quality problems – and this is why all the great product development and production companies do it.
- Keep tasks groomed within an OPL (open point list) or Kanban board, depending on how visual you like it and make burndown charts, showing how much work is still to be done to be able to track progress.
- Keep the important data transparent and visible. This helps the team focus. It can be anything, like a mission and vision board, a dashboard with key metrics, a screen about the current sprint or any other means of transmitting important information giving people guidance

- Measure only the meaningful things related to your track, which can show your progress towards the goal indicate the problems upfront. Measuring everything, or nothing are neither good ideas.
- Use online and offline digital tools and automate everything you can. If you cannot automate, provide the most possible manual aids to increase the efficiency of processes, e.g. a trigger matrix helping decision making.

#5·3·1 Trigger matrix for champions

Let us keep the spacewalk metaphor. To be able to leave planet Earth and become extraplanetary, we need a rocket or spaceship that takes us there. When planning the journey, we need to consider forces and other phenomenons, e.g. gravity, and radiation that make it harder to reach our destination. Startups are space pioneers, who need to build rockets and fight the elements trying to hinder the liftoff and the success of the journey.

This pioneer mindset can help HW startups win the game: keep the engineering team together, develop the product correctly, solve all the upcoming problems and overcome all the obstacles. We have made a tool for this, based on the D- and P-FMEA scoring system. When making a design- or process FMEA, the goal is to create a prioritized action list showing the problems you should solve first. Scoring there is based on points given for severity, occurrence, and detectability. You multiply these scores, and the result tells you whether you need to take any actions. In our tool we have applied exactly the same method, but with different factors.

We build a rocket. We create a plan and make the engine, then the fuel system, and we develop the landing system. For all the processes and for every task planned on your path, you can consider the following:

- Does the task or process have a healthy momentum or is it losing it? This is the **Engine.**
- Is the progress going at the same pace? Is it going much faster than other items? If we are too fast here, later if we need to change course, this will be a sunken cost. This is the **Fuel**.
- How important is this item? Is it a must to have? What kind of impact does it have on the business (model)? This is the **Landing system.**

All the three aspects can be scored on the scale of 1 to 5. The table on the next page summarizes how to rate these aspects, giving you some hints on each score for the different factors.

Rocket (drives us)

Aspect	Engine	Fuel	Landing system
Description	**Does the task or process have a healthy momentum or is it losing it?**	**Is the progress going at the same pace? Is it going much faster than other items? If we are too fast here, later if we need to change course, this will be a sunken cost.**	**How important is this item? Is it a must to have? What kind of impact does it have on the business (model)?**
1	Momentum there, task on track	Running together with other items	Feature with no or little direct effect on the business
2	Deliveries failing from time to time	A bit faster progress	Would be nice to have … later
3	Long term momentum-loss foreseeable	Starting to overgrow other tasks	Nice to have
4	Short term momentum-loss foreseeable	The progress of other tasks are running after this one. It makes them hurried and unfocused.	Must to have, customer wish. Important, but not essential.
5	Danger of becoming an anchor	Drains too many resources. If it stays so, it may lead to energy burnt unnecessarily.	It is a must to have with high priority.

When planning the rocket taking us to space, we need to consider some counterforces, like **Aerodynamic pressure**, **Gravity**, and **Radiation**. Using the same analogy here, you can have three types of task or items:

- Critical path items in the project are the ones, the delay in which results in the delay of the project. This is **Aerodynamic pressure.**
- Items that will cause a further delay. This is **Gravity**
- What is the impact of the problem, if not solved (in time). This is the **Radiation**

Again, the three aspects can be scored on the scale of 1 to 5 and the table on the next page summarizes how to rate these aspects, giving you some hints on each score for the different factors.

Aspect	Aerodynamic pressure	Counterforces (blocks us)	
		Gravity	Radiation
Description	Critical path items in the project are the ones, the delay in which results in the delay of the project.	Items that will cause a further delay.	What is the impact of the problem, when not solved (in time).
1	Not a critical item with no or few successors.	Item is getting close to deadline.	Easy fix.
2	Not a critical item with multiple successors.	Can be managed with some extra efforts.	Needs follow up.
3	Important item, but not on the critical path.	Can be managed with some extra resources.	Needs special attention.
4	Critical path item with important successors. Can cause latency.	Needs dedicated team to solve it.	Needs dedicated team to solve it.
5	Critical path item with high priority successors.	Further delay is not accepted.	The future of the project is in danger.

As you can see, every task, problem or backlog item can be categorized into either being a rocket part or a counterforce, based on the two tables above and you can score them on the scale from 1 to 5. If you multiply the three factors, the result is going to be your Northern Star, setting you the path, as you prioritize the factors from the biggest number to the smallest one. The higher the score is, the more focus, and urgency the task requires.

After the scoring is done, you can also categorize the items into different sets we call zones:

E x F x L or A x G x R		
	Zone	ToDo
1-19	OK	Track
20-49	Danger	Target
50-125	Death	Solve immediately

The first zone is the **OK zone**. Track these items! At the moment they are harmless, but this may change very quickly anytime. The next zone is the **Danger zone**. Target these tasks, and solve them, before they get into the **Death zone**, where you are near the chain of pivot or persevere meetings! Items in the death zone may result in the termination of the project, the end of the startup, major damage to the team, pivot, or other bad events.

We would like to spend some words on pivot. Pivot is pivot, with the same meaning as it has in other (SW) startups: Changing direction. Making a major change, e.g. change in value capture, business architecture, technology, zoom in or out, customer segment, or platform. The differences are made by the costs and the consequences. In SW startups you may just throw some lines of code out, change the tech stack, some service providers or the design. This is, of course, exaggerated and oversimplified, we know. Changing the tech stack or moving to another core system provider is a big deal, yet most of the SW companies can accomplish it without major issues.

In HW business, rapidly changing technology can ruin your whole business. The financial and timely pressure, or the stress caused by change of the specification due to the pivot can cost the life of the project, therefore the planning and preparation phases need to contain a risk analysis and feasibility study as deep as the Mariana Trench, which is updated constantly. Changing key technologies, suppliers, or a material category during the preparation for mass production just because you have not validated the customers' needsIt is too expensive and close to unacceptable in this industry and adding parts because it is nicer is also a no go in most of the cases. Planning and the replannings have to be so accurate, that even the idea of a major pivot should be forgotten. Micropivots may happen, but not after design freeze, and possibly not due to major change in HW.

#5·4 Make your unique framework

We could have listed hundreds of further tools too, but the idea was to give you an overview, an empty canvas, and some basic tools to start with. However, the tools applied can never be the only factors of success, it is always the result of choices, consequent use of the tools, and the focused work to reach your destination. We live in a time, when it is hard to choose from the wide range of digital tools extending our framework. You have a great number of SaaS (Software as a Service) to choose from., and we suggest you to consider having at least some of the online solutions, such as

- Communication tools
- Project management tools
- Teamwork tools
- Meeting tools
- Collaboration tools
- Effectivity tools
- ERPs (Enterprise Resource Planning), MESs (Manufacturing execution System), and other big company toys

The core elements of the framework and additional SaaSs all need to be a part of daily life, otherwise they will just be a waste of money and effort. Improper use of them is not their fault, nor ours, and not the providers'. It is your journey, your way, your choice. It is you, who should find the matching tools for the job to be done and tailor your own framework. To be able to create your own toolbar, you need to find out:

- Which job should the tools do?
- Who will use them, when and why?
- How frequently should you use the tools?
- When should you redesign your framework?
- What fits your team?
- What will bring the results?
- What is the professional background of the team?

All the questions arising during the planning process of your framework should target the roadmap of your project. You need to find a knob fitting the jacket and not a jacket fitting for the knob. In the next chapters we will help you understand the jacket by explaining the complexity of HW startups and the roadmap you need to plan.

#6 Introduction of complexity layers

In the previous chapters we introduced the framework that will serve you well on your journey. It is time to focus again on the goal and the road, which takes you there. Here we will introduce the four fundamental layers of hardware startups briefly, then in chapter #7 in more detail. In chapter #8 we are going to figure out how to find your path through this complexity and how to plan your own roadmap.

Where should we begin? There is no Stackoverflow where you can just post your questions and not only get your answers, but also the code that you can copy-paste into your software. Physical product development and production is a closed society of many participants, who gathered their knowledge piece by piece with tears and sweat. They also use a language that is difficult to understand if you do not have a corporate background. When you talk to industry experts about your hardware startup, it is hard to even understand what they are asking, not to mention that most of their answers will never make sense to you. How should you know if you pick the right supplier? Which machine is the best investment? How can you learn all of this? Can you learn it at all?
Even with enough theoretical knowledge, how will you get the experience? Is knowledge enough? Is experience overrated?

These and similar questions have pushed this book to come to life, complemented by all the failures we have seen over and over again, just because there was no manual for hardware startups. Because 'hardware is hard', as the famous investor phrase says.

The framework we built for depicting the differences between the two journeys is a visual layering of the different problems each startup has to solve during their lifetime.

Any startup has tons of problems (tasks) to tackle during their lifetime, but all of the problems can be classified into one of the following categories:

- Technical problems
- Business issues
- Staffing (People)
- Finance, mostly funding and cash-flow management

Let us call them layers. Layers, which are interrelated, influence each other in one way or another, making some decisons irrational if we do not consider their effects on each other.

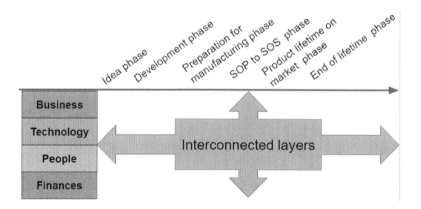

No matter if you are a software startup or a hardware company, your problems will most likely fit into one or more of these categories.

But what do these layers mean?

Well, technical problems are issues related to the product. Software code, user experience, integration, API and so on. If we want to break the layers down into smaller sublayers, we might come up with the front end, the back end, the app layers and the integration. At this simplified level, that's pretty much it, plus the hardware-related topics. Any of your technical problems fit into one of the above.

Business problems are related to pre-sales, post-sales, or marketing. You try to figure out whom to sell, how to sell, provide support once on board and keep them in the system to raise the lifetime value of customers. You also have to worry about logistics, or legal constraints, most of the time.

Staffing is related to all the problems that come with leading and managing people. You have to be able to forecast the needs of engineers, sales, and support staff in advance to be able to hire them in a timely manner.

Financing or funding is the part where you make money for the marketing, operations, and personnel costs. It can be planned, and apart from some fatal mistakes that might occur, the biggest risk is in the software team delivering late and the sales numbers lagging behind the expected results. Compared to the other risks of a hardware startup, this is a walk in the park, but more on that later.

If you look at your company in this way, you can already see that business and technical problems will result in forecasting the staffing needs and the three add up into the funding requirements. It is fairly easy to manage the cost side, even if the revenue side is risky at first. Still, the costs can be forecasted as most of the associated cost is infrastructure servicing the software and clients, and personnel costs.

It's not rocket science. Complex, but not complicated.

Now let's enter the hardware business and let's see how these layers look like for such a business.

#7 Depth of Layers

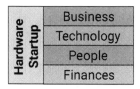

After the introduction of the four layers we are going to elabo-
rate on them one-by-one, showing you how deep they really
are. Imagine the startup itself as the trunk of a tree, on which
there are loads of trenches. The first and biggest separation is
shown by the four basic layers, Business, Technology, People,
and Finance, but the whole trunk is covered with smaller and
bigger trenches, which can remerge and separate, again and
again.

In the following, we will discuss each of the four main domains
to give you an insight into the real depth of them. The complexity within complexity is that almost every sublayer and topic is
connected to more than one of the other layers in the way we
have already mentioned. It is like the neural network of the brain,
where the individual neurons – or, in our case, the elements of
the plan – are connected to several others; and a single change
in one influences the behavior of the others. Turning back to
hardware startups, if we change the material of one part of
a product, it has an influence on the price, sourcing, assembly
method, manufacturing method of the part, quality requirements, customer experience, etc.

The next source of complication are these layers not being fixed: they may change based on your progress, the industry and numerous other external factors of the macro level. If you change a technology or pivot with the business model, it rearranges the layers and sublayers. The intensity or dominance of the layers will also change in the different phases a startup goes through, which, in most cases are the following

- Idea phase
- Development phase
- Preparation for production phase
- SOP (Start of production) to SOD (Start of delivery) phase
- Product lifetime on market phase
- EOL (End of Lifetime) phase

In the idea phase, the business layer is the dominant, while in the development phase technology takes the lead, but within technology, the sublayers also have their own dance. Production phase is again at a completely different level. This is the consequence of the rapid maturation of HW startups: from startup they need to grow to an engineering office, and from that on to a production company – all stages with different challenges and rapidly changing competence requirements.

In this chapter we are going to give you a base setup of the layers and some extra insights into them at the different phases of the HW startup life and its complexity. We will indicate the interrelations with a bracket after each item, indicating the layers involved, for example: *Feature list [B, T], where feature list is related to the business and the technology layers, since it influences both of them and if the feature list changes, it has an effect on the business model and also on the technology used, design, and quality planning.*

To give you a quick overview of how all the four layers may interact in each phase of the life of a startup, let's see a simplified draft of how an idea can evolve to become a startup:

- An idea pops up: a customer has a problem and a solution should be provided.
- **Validation** [B, T] ensures product market fit
- In the development phase validation continues, the product, the business model and the production model gets a shape
- During production preparation **sourcing** [B, T, F], **logistic** [B, F], **production** [B, T, F, P] and **sales processes** [B, F] become fixed
- After the **start of the production** [T, F, P] the business and the product reach maturity all the companies wish for; **start of delivery** [B, F] begins.
- **Product lifecycle** [B, T, F] is running with all the **compliance** [B, T, F] and **maintenance** [B, T, F] topics, while **new product development** [B, T, F] is already running for the next model.
- **End of lifetime** [F] for the product, new product lifecycle already started, this one starts to phase out.

As you could see above, there is almost no item taking effect in only one of the four layers – most of them influence at least two, but usually more areas, which shows perfectly how complex HW startups can be. In the following section we are going to highlight and discuss some of the most important items of each layer, which have not been discussed yet – and list numerous others also related to the given layer.

#7·1 Business

The business layer provides the spinal cord and the skeleton of the whole startup. The bones of the skeleton are the base of the company, the way the startup creates value to the customers, why it is able to do so, and how the founders and the team make everything happen.

Let's discuss the major topics making the initial depth of the business layer. We have already discussed some of these topics, such as validation, new set of tools and problems and their solutions in depth in #3. The remaining business-heavy topics are sourcing, logistics, compliance and quality assurance, which we are going to cover now.

#7·1·1 Sourcing

At the beginning of the project, you will most probably buy everything from local stores, online shops, or small distributors to cut the costs, but the goal is to build a network of reliable suppliers sooner or later, who can serve you in time with quality materials, and products.

This sounds easy, but to be able to create your own network of suppliers, you need to be aware of a wide range of parameters determining whom it is the best to cooperate with. First of all, you need to know what you would like to buy. You need all the customer needs turned into technical specifications. This is the minimum requirement to even be able to negotiate with the supplier. You should also have an idea on the amount of materials, off the shelf products or parts made to specification you will need in a month, in a year, or for the whole product lifetime.

After giving them the information they need, suppliers will give you an offer, usually containing the following data:

- Items they can deliver (item name, item number)
- Minimum order quantity (MOQ)
- Price
- They often give a list of MOQs and prices related to them:
  - 1000 pcs → 4,5 €
  - 2000 pcs → 4,46 €
  - 10 000 pcs → 4,35 €

This means, if you buy more, you can get a better price. From this point on this starts to be a logistical and financial question as well, since storing components costs money and takes place in your warehouse/storage.

- Lead time
- This is a critical question, especially at the time this book is being written. In general, we can talk about short- and long lead time components, which you need to consider, when ordering the different items. However, lead times can increase a lot (2-4 weeks → 24-26 weeks) due to unforeseen events, as has happened to all the electronics, plastic raw materials and screws in the past few years.

Suppliers may give you a possibility to make frame orders – a special order, where you ask for a bigger quantity, and freeze the conditions, in most of the cases the price, for a longer period. Frame orders are good for securing the availability of critical materials, and giving security to the suppliers by promising that you will buy a bigger demand. This is basically a form of risk mitigation, taking the obligation of buying the goods/material, and a good way of asking for better pricing or conditions. This is useful in at least two cases. First, when you have limited storage space, therefore you would like to order the goods to be shipped to you in smaller batches, spread during a longer period, e.g. business year. Second, when the raw material should be ordered in a bigger amount, due to various reasons, e.g. volatile prices, or material availability. Usually, metals belong to this second category. Copper, and aluminum are good examples of prices following the stock exchange, therefore are highly volatile – frame orders provide some level of security in these cases.

At this point, there is a conflict of interest between the two parties. I often face cases, when the manufacturing company asks quotes for the yearly quantity and the MOQ is optimized for that. For startups it is usually pretty hard to plan so much ahead, but from the perspective of the manufacturing company this means the reduction of obsolete risk and excess stock (which is in fact a financing issue). On the other hand, startups as customers often ask quotes for the project quantity (which may be enough for 3-5 years or more), as this way they can show bigger purchasing power and get better price offers – but this lacks considering the interest of the manufacturer. Both methods may be and are used in real life, but sooner or later compromises have to be made, as the interests should be aligned otherwise the risk and the price differences are going to cause issues at both parties.

The request for quotation (RFQ) process related to materials, parts or products is easier if you are prepared to answer the upcoming questions, such as

- Place of use
- Conditions under which the item is going to be used
- Requirements (e.g. heat resistance, conductibility, coating, etc.)
- Specifications

Do not forget that the core competence of suppliers is supply, not product development. Of course, customer care and support have to be part of the price you pay, but do not fall into the misconception of thinking that their support and resources are limitless.

When you choose to work with a contract manufacturer, or any other kind of big company, it is important to know that they have strict rules, e.g. for payment terms. So, big companies take big and reliable, financially stable suppliers, who can also supply in big quantities. They are usually not so flexible, but cheap, and the goods are more often in stock in bigger quantities. Also, the lead time can be reasonably short, since the big suppliers or distributors often have stock, or you can contact the manufacturer directly. This is a fact, or if you prefer, a status quo. Small suppliers cannot really live with conditions like net 30-, 60- or 90-day payment from the end of the month. This would kill their cash flow, due to the long period of not getting their money. Usually they do not have this size of financial stability, but they are flexible and more helpful. They take the time to help and support you, until it is affordable for them.

The goal should be to set up a reliable supplier base triggered by the maturity of the product development, and the approaching start of production.

#7·1·2 Logistics

Logistics include every movement not only on the supply chain – from transporting raw material to delivering finished goods –, but also the internal logistics of parts, materials, and goods within the production plant. This means that logistics is a complicated topic influenced by numerous different factors, like the circumstances of transportation and legal requirements of different countries; and including some critical points, such as understanding different incoterms, warehouse types, and stock.

Transportation times and costs

Different shipment types can influence price and lead time heavily. Air shipment is fast, but it can cost 8-10€/kg (or, in case of low-weight packages, you may pay for volume, not weight). Trucks and trains are much cheaper, but you need to count with 4-8 weeks of transportation time in the optimal case. On the road, the size of the truck and delivery company influences the price. There are 24h and 48h delivery express services if you need them, but of course, they are priced according to the time pressure. Transportation on water is the least costly among the different forms available, but also the slowest and the most exposed to weather conditions – which makes it also riskier to choose.

These are the so-called optimal cases, but in terms of transportation many things can go wrong: a load of goods may get stuck on the sea or the track, a truck may have technical issues, but we have also seen huge shipping companies go bankrupt. To minimize the problems occurring from such cases, you need to manage your stock levels wisely.

Stock

Optimizing the stock level is critical. One of the seven wastes (originating from the Toyota Production System) is overstock. It does not only require storage space, but makes your money stuck as well. Financing excess stock is not rational. The opposite end of the scale is when you run out of parts. A minimum level of goods should be set, which triggers the next sourcing round (considering the lead times, of course). Stock level and value have to be optimized and controlled. You can set KPIs (Key Performance Indicator) for that, such as MOQ/Stock ratio. The main point is to understand the demand of your manufacturing process and the supply process of your supply chain.

Safety stock

Safety stock is a special kind of stock to cover problematic times. This is especially important in the case of long-lead-time components (LLC) sourced from the Far East, and finished goods. This has to be regulated in a contract or agreement in some ways. It is a good practice to categorize the parts and materials in commodities, e.g. packaging material, fasteners, raw material, made-to-specification goods, or off-the-shelf parts. In these categories, the lead time, price, and other factors can help identify the ones requiring priority. This provides guidance to set the right safety stock levels.

The main goal of stock management is to support continuous production and serve the demand of different items, e.g. service parts,while keeping the stock level as low as possible, not wasting money and storage capacity.

Warehouse

You can store the parts, raw materials and finished goods in warehouses owned or rented by you, your customer, or your supplier, but there is also a special type of warehouse called consigned warehouse.In this case you have an external warehouse at (or near) your supplier and your customer pays for you (=you can send the invoice) after taking the goods from the warehouse. In normal cases, you are billing right after delivery, or, in rare cases, in advance. Of course, you can also be on the customer's side, and experience the same process from the other point of view too, but in that case, the essence remains the same.

Incoterms

The word itself comes from International Commercial Terms. This is the determination of 'who pays for what, who takes the risk, and what each party is responsible for' in the case of sending goods from A to B. These terms are changing regularly, but here you can see the current regulation:

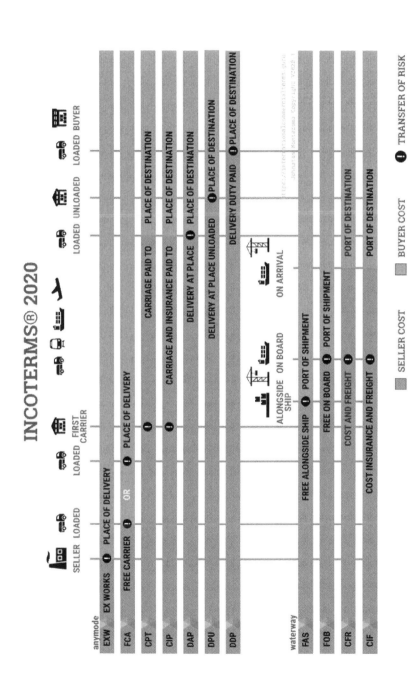

INCOTERMS® 2020

Companies from the Far East often give FOB, where they bring goods to the port, but you need to organize the shipment, or they offer you EXW parity, where you organize the transport from their warehouse to yours. Suppliers near you give DAP, DDP or FCA prices in most of the cases, where the goods are delivered to your place. These differences influence the cost over the base price and it is definitely something you should consider through the whole supply chain, up to your customers. You can set different percentages in your price calculation for transport, e.g. 1-3% for FCA, 5-10% for EXW and FOB, but, of course, the weight of the goods, the packaging and quantity are going to influence these percentages. However, it is still easier to handle things this way, than recalculating your prices with every transport.

Customs

At one point of time, you will ship your product outside your country, hopefully globally. But probably from the very beginning, you need to buy parts originating from other countries, which means import and export are a crucial part of your processes, which means, cannot avoid dealing with custom clearance. There are different custom fees for different types of goods, which may also differ by country. You need to be aware of these before doing or buying anything, since customs will influence your costs and processes in numerous ways. Within-country or regional purchases are mostly not so complicated, but if, as an EU or US company, you buy something from the Far East for example, or from any country outside yours (which means outside EU, if you are an EU member), you cannot open it until it is released, because it is dutiable, otherwise the local tax offices can penalize you, or even shut your company down.

#7·1·3 Quality

If we talk about quality in the Business layer, we mean the value provided to the customer, including

- Quality of the product
- Quality of service
- Quality of materials
- User experience
- Customer satisfaction
- Brand promise
- and, of course, the management of claims, technical problems during the product lifetime.

Customers do not consider business complexity and production methods, they are not going to think about specifications and pivots. The only thing they care about is to solve their own problem by the product you produce. They will not evaluate the quality of the materials; they judge by their perception on whether the product is serving their needs and the only thing that matters is the perceived experience on functionality, which is rather subjective.

On top of it all, customers do not care about complications and material shortages. They do not consider the costs of keeping a larger stock either – they only focus on getting their own product when they need it. Also, when problems occur, they will not consider any of these factors in most of the cases, only the harm done to them, which they seek remedy for. If their complaints are handled properly, there is a possibility that they keep a positive opinion about the company, but if they perceive any form of mistreatment or injustice, the image of the corporation may be completely ruined.

This may be the hardest part of your business: giving the customers what they wish, look for, and need, again and again, but still: without customers there is no business, so we need to always try to make the best out of it!

#7·1·4 Some other items related to business

- Validation
  - Hypothesis list [B, T]
  - Customer persona [B, T, F, P]
    - For Whom it is built [B]
    - Who will use it [B]
    - Customer [B]
    - Customer engagement [B]
  - Problem [B]
    - Problem interview [B]
  - Solution [B]
    - Solution interview [B]
  - MXY [B, T]
  - VP – Value proposition[B]
  - USP – Unique selling point/proposition[B]
  - Business Model Canvas [B, F]
  - Design thinking, Service thinking [B, T]
- Idea→Product
  - Feature list [B, T]
    - Must have [B, T]
    - Nice to have [B, T]
    - No AV (added value) [B, T]

- Customer experience (CX) [B, T]
- User stories [B, T]
- Epic backlog [B, T]
- Cost of knowledge and experience [B, T, F, P]
- Innovation adaptation curve [B]
  - Chasm [B]
- Internal packaging [B, T]
- Packaging [B, T]
- Business plan [B, F]
- Financial plan [B, F]
- Pricing model [B, F]
- Business model [B, F]
- Brand [B]
- Documentation [B, T]
- Pricing strategy [B, F]
- Go to market strategy [B]
- Legal [B]
  - Contracts and terms [B]
- Liability [B, T]
- Domain knowledge [B, T, P]
- User's manual [B, T, F]
- Departments, functions [B, F, P]
-
- Production
  - Supply chain [B]
    - Sourcing / purchasing [B]
    - Selection of suppliers [B]
    - Supplier development [B]
    - Slow moving [B, F]
    - Obsolete [B, F]
    - MOQ [B, T, F]
    - Country of origin [B, F]

- Incoterms [B, F]
-
- LT of components [B]
-
  - Payment terms [B, F]
  - SW solutions [B, T, P]
  - Production model [B, T, F]
    - Direct labor [B, T, F, P]
    - Automation [B, T, F]
- Semiautomatic lines [B, T, F]
  - Preparation to production
    - 0-series [B, T, F]
    - Engineering series 0-X [B, T]
  - Production batch size [B, T, F]
  - Production optimisation [B, T, F]
  - Proof of concept [B, T]
  - Proof of process [B, T]
  - Hands on experience [B, T]
  - Start of production [B, T, F]
  - Ramp-up [B, T, F]
  - Start of sales [B, T, F]
  - Start of delivery [B, T, F]
  - Scaling production [B, T, F]
  - Transfer of production [B, T, F]
  - EOL components [B, F]
  - Forecast [B, F]
  - Change management [B, T]
  - Marketing [B, F]
  - Quality [B, T, F]
    - Quality costs [B, F]
    - First pass yield or Nor right first time [B, T, F]
  - Investment + ROI [B, F]

- Service and maintenance [B, T, F]
- Product on the market
  - IP rights [B, T]
  - Environmental impact [B, T]
  - Environmental footprint [B, T]
  - Product lifecycle management [B, T]
  - Product liability [B, T]
  - Customer claim [B, T, F]
  - Sales [B, F]
    - Presales [B, F]
    - Aftersales [B, F]
    - Sales plan [B, F]
    - Sales channels [B]
- Distribution [B]
  - Customer lifetime value [B]
  - Sustainable quality [B, T]
  - Voice of the customer [B]
  - Logistics [B, T, F]
    - Last mile carrier [B]
    - Excess stock [B, F]
    - Incoterms (again) [B]
  - Product recall [B, T, F]
  - Emission [B, T, F]
- End of product lifetime [B, T, F]
  - Recycling [B, T, F]
  - Development of next product [B, T, P, F]

As you can see, the points we listed in business are not business items only. The influence of the items on each other makes things more complex, as you will also see in the Technology layer.

#7·2 Technology

If the business layer was the skeleton, the technology layer is the muscular system moving the whole body, made up of tiny little parts interrelated and interacting with each other. This topic is huge. Defining all the layers, sublayers, and their connection is almost impossible; and the list could go a lot more levels deeper, believe me, until you define every screw torque, every material, and all the spare parts you need to design, specify, check, or produce. The worst mistake you can make is not paying enough attention in time to all the crucial points; it will cost a lot later, as the following diagram shows.

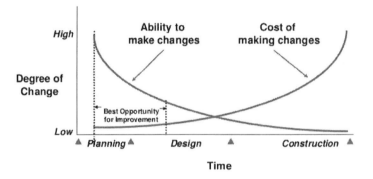

There are some items from the very long list of technology items that should be elaborated, but this here is just a starter, an over-view, nothing else. Please read it in such a way, that you remind yourself after each major point, that this is just the surface that could still be scratched in a digestible way.

Please note: taking all items and describing them well is im-possible to handle in one book!

Here we will start the introduction with possible production models and then talk about compliance and quality, but as you will see at the end of the chapter, there are numerous other items making technology so complex and complicated.

#7·2·1 Production possibilities — In-house or outsourcing?

When it comes to production, you have multiple options to get your product manufactured: you can build up your own production plant, or you can outsource it under numerous different conditions. It looks like a simple decision, but wait for it! The devil is in the details. It is not an easy choice, but probably, if you have capital from an investor, they may already have a clear idea on how they prefer the production to be set up. If not, it is you who needs to make this decision.

In-house

Building up in-house production is a heavy topic. It takes a lot of investment in capital and takes way more time than one might think at first sight. If you have time to scale up, it could work, but if you need a rapid scaling up in output (meaning 1-2 years instead of 3-5) , then it is not the way we suggest you go.

Knowledge and human resources
In case you would like to choose this path, you will need specific knowledge in production, logistics, lean methodologies, quality assurance, process development, sourcing and numerous other areas, which is, of course, not a one-man job, but requires a team owning all the necessary skills. Therefore, human resources are

another crucial factor of in-house production: you can only do all the things right if you have the necessary amount of well-qualified workforce, who is able to fulfill the different tasks without constantly being observed and guided. As we have already emphasized, it is not a functioning model, where the founder(s) are the owners of every knowledge – and exceeding a certain level of complexity it is not even possible to be competent in everything after all.

Production line

This, in itself, is hard enough to achieve, but if you are building a product, you cannot do it on the kitchen table. You need a line helping the workers and supporting them to have everything in place to keep up good quality. To be able to set up a production plant, machines, tools and equipment, e.g. gauges, fixtures are also needed, which requires huge, but carefully considered investment.

A smaller manual line can cost 1-300K €, with screwdrivers, testers, special fixations, ESD protection, tablets for documentation, and we could go on, while an automated line can easily cost 0,5-3M €.

You will need all the equipment and tools to be there for the people building your products. Supermarket quality crimpers, pliers, and screwdrivers are not an option. A good electric screwdriver with torque settings option can cost 300-1000€, and you will probably need 3-7 of them.

The more you help the manufacturing process, the less quality cost you will have, occurring from customer claims or scrap generated during the production process. The cost of these jugs, gauges and fixtures may be around 200-1000 €. You will need more of them than you think! What was your initial number in your financial plan?

Technologies

To be able to do these investments right, you need to be aware of the technologies used in the industry and you will have to choose the one fitting your purpose the best. Ultrasonic welding, gluing, potting, soldering, welding on the line needs extra investment. 10-80K € can be easily spent. Testers, especially optical testers, are also costly. These technologies can be expensive, but also they are robust and reliable, and often also inevitable.

Engineering builds

Building products, refining them, and finding out how to produce them are called engineering builds. Of course, there are other, similar descriptions but the meaning is the same: proofing something in the different stages of product development, and making it ready to be produced in bigger quantities. Engineering builds may have different aims, such as proof of concept, testing parts, technologies, trying out assembly, finding out what fixtures are necessary, proof of production method, etc.

Engineering builds will become cheaper with product maturity, thanks to the readiness of production equipment, requiring fewer engineering work hours, and the availability of mass production materials instead of small quantity purchases from webshops. Still, you can count with about 2-2,5 times the mass production price at the end, before SOP. In spite of the costs, engineering builds cannot be avoided – you need to plan with this extra effort and cost.

Prototyping

There are various technologies we call prototyping. Here let us define prototyping as production technologies – both additive and subtractive – where you receive a quick result. 3D printing is fast, making an injection molding tool out of aluminum is also fast, and applying materials easier to use speeds the process up too, and though these solutions are slightly different from the final product, you can test certain functions before investing in more complicated and expensive tools and materials.

However, the cost of speed is high. Proto tools for plastics, 3D printed parts, individually manufactured or special parts, proto PCBAs (Printed Circuit Board Assembly) are as expensive as gold (or some of the cryptocurrencies these days), so you will change them to technologies suitable for mass production and incurring a significantly lower piece price. The projected piece price will reduce with every engineering build, since the concept and used parts will become finer and finer, and the sourcing more standardized.

However, no matter how high-tech prototyping technologies may be, they can also mislead you. 3D printing at the moment is not equivalent to injection molding regarding material properties and durability of the parts. Also, you can create shapes with 3D printing, which cannot be done with other technologies, especially in the case of metal 3D printing. Size tolerance is not the same, the repeatability of the quality over bigger quantities either. Maybe the day will come, when it will change, but at the moment technologies applied for prototyping are rarely suitable for mass production.

Maintenance

When you have already set up everything, there is still one crucial factor you cannot overlook: maintenance cycles. No matter how developed your production plant is, if you do not pay enough attention to continuous maintenance and improvement, it can cost you a lot later, when you have to spend fortunes on repairing machines or replacing them, and you cannot serve customers due to a sudden halt in production.

As you can see, it is highly complex and expensive to set up a production plant, therefore before starting doing anything, you need to evaluate the business case for this big investment and decide whether it is worthwhile and feasible to make it at all.

Outsourcing

In this book we will focus a lot on the outsourcing methods too, since we assume that, as a startup, you need to focus on the most cost-efficient way of growth, which is expected not just by your customers but also by your investors. When it comes to outsourcing, the degree may vary from partial involvement to almost completely relying on external parties to produce, but here we have collected the three most common models, CM, ODM and OEM. These are the three major types of manufacturing models, but, of course, the boundaries are not really sharp. We have seen CM++, ODM-, ODM+ companies as well. Also, the degree of support may change from company to company, depending on the organizational and national culture. Please contact us if you need more information on this topic!

CM model

CM stands for contract manufacturing. In this case you give the manufacturer all the documentation, you pay for the equipment and every other on-time-cost and they manufacture your product in the form and volume you ask for. In most cases, they do not have the engineering capacity to develop for you, or if they do, their knowledge is less specific, as they may not have deep knowledge of the type of product you have. Since they deal with a big variety of products, they are universal, and therefore it is a false wish that they are experts in every technology up to the deepest detail, even if they have this written on their website. And this is the reason why they are relatively cheap – they can do the job in high quality, but you need to be highly involved in the development and provide them with clear specifications to avoid dead ends and pivots.

As for the type, you can find any shape and size of CM-s, from manual assembly to fully automatic assembly lines, but you need to be well aware of what you are going to need to be able to cooperate efficiently.

ODM model

ODM stands for original design manufacturing. In this model the manufacturers can design your product and also manufacture it, if you find the right partner having the expertise on the fields necessary. There are specialized ODMs, so with some effort you can easily find one with the right experience. Location, price level, and customer care will also vary company by company, which can, of course influence your decision as well.

If you find the right partner, it can make your development process much easier too, as they can already suggest the parts and technology they have good experience with. This, of course, may be a drawback as well, since they also prefer to stay in their comfort zone and use the good old parts and methods, even if you have different – and probably better –, innovative ideas.

This method is generally more expensive than CM, but it also depends on the level of contribution of your own company to the process – co-development is also an option, where the development tasks are shared between the customer and the manufacturer. The higher the added value of the manufacturer side is, the higher the one-time cost (engineering HR cost) and the piece-price are going to be, since the hourly assembly price also needs to cover the work of the engineering department.

OEM model

OEM stands for original equipment manufacturing. In this case the manufacturer makes and sells products, which other com-panies can buy and build in their own products as a part. This is, of course, the most expensive model, but has its benefits as well, since you do not need a development department with tens of engineers, designers, developers, and so on.

Manufacturers could also have whitelabel products, which you can buy and introduce on the market as yours, under your own brand, but these are special cases, where the customer clearly has less freedom in innovation, therefore this is not the most common model in the startup environment.

Expectations versus reality

On one side, there is a startup (maybe in the storming or forming phase) with young, agile, motivated people. "We will do it", they say loud and (sometimes also) clear. On the other side, there is a company with often 30+ years of experience and rules, and policies carved in stone. You cannot teach them new things, you cannot bring in new methods, they have already been doing it as they do, when you had not even been able to speak. This is the status quo in its purest form.

Their hair will fall out hearing your wishes and behind your back they will say (with some right basis of course) that you have no idea how it works and you should come back down to Earth. Be open, be prepared, and never let your guard down! You cannot change them, but you can go with reduced friction on your common journey if you try to mutually consider each other's expectations, needs and interests.

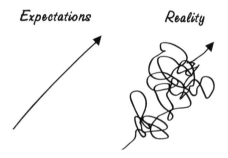

A production company needs production load, crystal clear documentation, and precise change management. The more, the better – this is true in specification, but, of course, not in changes. Efficiency in production with limited flexibility is what you will see in every single process, also those far away from the workshop floor. Large manufacturing companies have their processes and these processes keep them alive. They know how to optimize their shifts, capacity, storage and so on; and once it is set, they do not wish to modify it every second day. They think you have a supplier manual and all the quality documents and requirements written, so they can easily align.

Design freeze means a perfect product, when you have already taken care of DFM (design for manufacturing), considering all the manufacturing processes necessary with all the major rules applied. The expectation towards you is to have a frozen design and everything finished, so they have nothing to do, but manufacture and ship the goods. This is their core activity, keep this in your mind!

As a startup, you most probably do not know all the manufacturing processes, since this amount of domain knowledge takes 20+ years to get gathered and at that point, many of them are already obsolete. This puts you in a handicapped situation from the manufacturer perspective, since you do not own the experience they do, however, this does not mean that your ideas would be less valuable, never forget that!

Cultural differences may make it even more complicated to get on the same side of the river. Some manufacturers, for example, always say yes to everything, even if they know the realization of certain things may meet serious obstacles, as this is simply in their company or national culture. On the contrary, there are companies and countries, where they constantly say 'no, this is impossible', and then, in the end, they do it in more than acceptable quality.

What you can expect from these companies is good mass production, but till reaching that point, be prepared to invest three times more energy in the project than you think now. Our suggestion here is to hire not just juniors, but good, experienced people as well. Learn as much as possible from your partners, but at the same time always question the things you hear or see, be critical, but never loud! You can stretch them – in the coaching and not the torture way –, but you need to stretch your people more. You are the new kid on their playground, even though they are kind of dinosaurs sometimes, as you may think. Just check back on their expectations and make some thoughts on how far you are from design freeze for each and every part of your assembly. And do not forget, you have one big project, your child, but their people have more projects to work on simultaneously!

#7·2·2 Documentation and compliance

We keep on mentioning quality requirements again and again, you might think, but our opinion is that they cannot be mentioned often enough. You do not want to pay for scrap parts and products not working, neither do your customers, nor your manufacturer. The requirements should always be realistic and defined and all parties should do their best to be able to meet them. Scrap will occur anyway, that is the reality, but it can be reduced and all possible actions should be taken to avoid it. Reducing scrap is going to be parallel with the learning curve: the more you know, the less mistakes you make. The most important thing to keep in mind is to solve the systematic problems, not the symptoms!

Documentation

Documentation is the heart and soul of everything: it includes all the written documents providing information about the product to the team, the manufacturers and the customers, covering all the tiniest details making sure everything is made and assembled as planned. This is the most important form of communication among the parties in the HW environment, the bible, the code of conduct for all involved.

Nothing can be more disturbing for a manufacturer, than the missing documentation. Engineers, quality people, and sourcing are using this daily. This is their life potion. The lack of proper documentation may lead to mistakes, misunderstandings – and therefore scrap, which everyone would like to avoid.

Documentation may appear in many forms serving different purposes, which add up to one complete entity describing every single piece and step of manufacturing and assembling a product – ensuring that everyone knows and understands everything the same way, down to the last tiny screw.

Manuals

Manuals tell people how to act, use the machines, pieces, parts and the products; they provide the process and flow of operation. Assembly, testing and inspection manuals and control plans provide the daily assurance for good quality. If made with care and available in time, they can save costs, scrap, human resource, working hours and other resources over time.

BOM

The bill of material is the structured list of the built-in components and their quantities. This is essential. You cannot believe how much it is.

2D drawings, 3D models

Your partner needs to understand what your product looks like and how it is built-up to be able to plan the manufacturing process. One picture says more than a thousand words. This is especially true if the 3D model is good and the 2D drawing contains all the measures, tolerances, and other data, such as the surface structure. Clear drawings and models can save hours of explanations and unnecessary rounds of failed production incurring tons of scrap. Be visual, be specific!

Specification

Even the simplest off-the-shelf part has at least a datasheet, which is crucial to source or manufacture the right part. Buying a screw, which is a little bit larger, or from a weaker material than necessary may ruin the whole process, which, then, you need to start all over again. It is your responsibility to specify your customer needs on every single detail to be turned into parameters and properties; this is how manufacturers and suppliers are going to know how to serve you the best. If you cannot tell them exactly what you need, they cannot find it out!

Change management

We have already spoken about changes. Once again, this is a crucial point. A small change in a method or material may result in numerous changes in all the documentation mentioned above, and you have to make sure that these changes reach all the parties involved in the most informative way, to, again, avoid misunderstandings – and scrap. Following up on which the previous version was, which the new one is and how they differ is crucial. The more information, the better.

The most important question here is the impact of the change. You need to determine how and which processes and parts the change is going to impact and how, and make all the decisions – ranging on a really wide span. What are the costs of the change? Is it worth making them? What is going to happen to the current stock? Will you throw it out, or will you use it up? How should you make the change visible? Should you implement new item codes or add-ons on previous ones? Should special labels be made to make the change obvious to everyone? And this could go on forever, depending on what kind of changes you would like to make and how big they are.

It is easy to see that any change generates a flow of questions, which need to be handled the right way in order to avoid havoc in the processes. This is even more important if you are running a production company, since the changes may be more expensive, therefore their impacts are larger and longer.

Certifications

To make things even more complicated, there are numerous standards and legal obligations to keep. These things sound like the unnecessary evil, but can cause serious issues, when not dealt with. Think about them in time!

REACH for example stands for Registration, Evaluation, Authorisation, and Restriction of Chemicals is one of the most important environmental regulations of the European Union. The REACH list contains all the restricted substances and those of high concern, which you may use and store only other certain conditions, meeting the strict security requirements. RoHS is a more specific regulation, which stands for Restriction of Hazardous Substances and lists the items banned in electronics. This is not just for your own safety, but that of those producing and using your product – and also the whole environment around us, when it comes to production processes. Be responsible, be compliant!

CE (Chartered Engineer) certificate is a marking applied on the Extended European Markets, which ensures that the products under this label meet a set of high levels of safety, health and environmental requirements and therefore are entitled to be sold without any restrictions on the countries of the given market.

Compliance, transportation, safety and other certifications may vary by country and region, the most important thing is to make sure you are aware of the ones applying to you and your product – not only in the country of production, but also in those, where you are selling.

Certification bodies need at least 4-6 weeks, but sometimes even longer for some expensive, but necessary certifications, which may also give you an extra round on rethinking your product. Even if you are optimistic, you cannot consider all the requirements, you simply cannot know all of them. This is why you need certification bodies, who are not to make your life more complicated, but to support you in meeting the requirements, which are a must if you want your product to arrive on the market. Plan accordingly, as much as you can!

#7·2·3 Some other items related to technology

- Validation [B, T]
  - Product validation [B, T]
  - Process validation [B, T]
  - Production validation [B, T]
  - Success metrics [B, T]
- Development on
  - Material level [T]
  - Part level [T]
  - Component level [T]
  - Subassy level [T]
  - System level [T]
- Development (process)
  - Component design [B, T]
  - System design [B, T]
  - Specification [B, T]
  - SW
    - Front End
    - Back End
    - Embedded SW [T]
    - To all three above the used technology, necessary HW and environmental requirements are sublayers, that have also sublayers.
    - Platform
    - Architecture
      - Tech stack [T]
    - Quality assurance on SW side
    - SW development [T]
    - SW testing [T]
    - SW validation [T]
    - Traceability Sw [T]

- Embedded SW [T]
- Production line SW [T]
- FE SW [T]
- Sprints [T]
- Daily scrum [T]
- Backend infrastructure [T]
  - HW
    - Materials
    - Processes
    - Technologies
    - DFMA [T] (Design for manufacturing and assembly)
    - DFM [T]
    - Design freeze [B, T]
    - Assembly
  - Integration [B, T]
  - Special technologies [T]
  - Industry best practice [T]
  - Feasibility [T]
    - Feasibility study [B, T]
    - Feasibility update [B, T]
  - Value chain planning [B, T]
  - Value chain mapping [B, T]
  - Prototyping
  - User/Process journey map
  - Documentation
    - Change management
    - Drawings
  - Quality planning
    - Flow chart [T]
    - Control plan [T]
    - P-FMEA [T]

- D-FMEA [T]
- Field test [T]
- Robust design [T]
- Simulation [T]
- Testing [T]
- Measurement [T]
- Special certifications
  - Health
  - Safety
  - Transport
  - Used materials
  - Legal requirements
- Validation [T], and Compliance [B, T]
  - REACH, ROHS [T]
  - CE rating [T]
  - FDA rating [T]
  - Tolerance chain [T]
  - IP rating [T]
- Production
  - Manufacturing model [T]
  - Ergonomics [T]
  - Production line [T]
  - Production equipment [T]
  - Production plannig [T]
  - Process control [T]
  - Jigs [T]
  - Fixtures [T]
  - Gauges [T]
  - Certificates [T]
  - Location [B, T]
  - Quality assurance
    - Right KPIs [B, T]

- Part approval [B, T]
- Production approval [B, T]
- Process approval [B, T]
- Product approval [B, F]
- Incoming goods inspection
- Supplier Quality assurance
- Production quality and Process engineering
  - Traceability
  - Quality check after production steps
- Outgoing and finished good quality assurance
- Claim handling
- Testing
  - Method
  - Metrics and measures
  - Equipment
  - KPIs and parameters
- Quality requirements [B, T]
- Flow chart [T]
- Control plan [T]
- P-FMEA [T]
- D-FMEA [T]
- Health and safety [T]
- ESD [T]
- Hazardous materials [T]
- Cpk, Cmk [T]
  - Production process
    - Workplaces
    - Ergonomics
    - Work safety requirements
    - Equipment
  - Supermarket [T]
  - JIT [T]

- (SW) Update [T]
- Maintenance plan [T]
- Lean production
  - Production line balancing [T]
  - Value stream map
  - Material flow [T]
  - Reducing wastes

#7·3 People

In Chapter #3 we have already mentioned numerous ways in which human behavior can affect a startup, but there are still a lot to discuss here. Previously, we have mainly focused on personal characteristics, which may bring up issues in a startup; discussing ego-issues, risk taking and biases mainly. We have also suggested possible ways of improvement, which may lead to solutions, such as building resilience and improving communication, team-working skills and trust within the team.

Now, at the people layer we are going to take a more process-driven approach by focusing on three main areas:

- Founding a HW startup
- Hiring for a HW startup
- Leading, and managing a HW startup

Going through these stages, we are going to highlight some important aspects

#7·3·1 Founding a HW startup

Many people think that founding a startup is all about having an idea and finding some cool people to realize it. Do not let yourself be blinded by the initial enthusiasm: it is way more complicated than that! There are a number of important decisions determining the future life of your startup, which have to be made already at this stage. You not only have to find the people you are going to work with, you also need to determine the optimal number and person of the individuals you involve and share the obligations, responsibilities and the risk too. If these decisions are not made and clarified towards all parties at the birth of the startup already, information gaps and misunderstandings may lead not only to arguments and personal stress, but also the parting of the founding team and probably even the end of an otherwise promising project.

Number of founders

It is never easy to determine how many founders can manage a startup the most efficiently – as you can see, a hardware startup requires a significantly wider span of core competencies than a regular SW startup. Are you going to need them all as a founder from the very first step? The answer can be both yes and no. From investors' perspective the best-case scenario is to have a great team with all the competencies and experience. For them, this is the least risky option. Is it also the least risky for the startup itself? The answer to this question is not even close to yes.

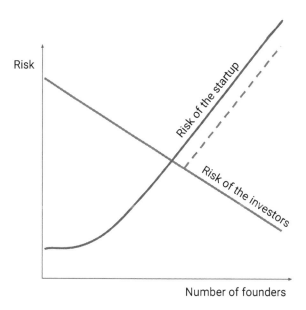

From a financial perspective, feeding such a big starting team is not exactly the 2 pizza 1 coke quick order: wages and taxes may reach the skies if we would like to have a team member for every competency at the beginning. The more people, the more costs – which a startup with limited funds can rarely afford. Also, the world has a shortage of industry experts and there is hardly any deal making them decide on a volatile, risky future. Engineers are not famous for their risk tolerance.

Besides the financial aspects there are the decision-making and management factors as well. Two heads are better than one when it comes to deciding about the future of the startup, but by the number of founders, the risk of unreachable alignment also increases – even though this aspect is somehow rarely discussed during investment rounds.

There are also the benefits of a core team with diverse knowledge. They can plan and calculate not only with high-level technological problems, but also work on the fine details from the very beginning. This can be a huge benefit, but as we can see, a deadweight and an extreme financial burden at the start of the journey.

To put it short, you always need to be aware of the financial possibilities you have – but also consider the decision making and crucial competencies you are going to need and try to set the number of founders based on these factors. We suggest having at least one senior project manager in the core team, who has seen enough of product development and start-of-production projects to know the potential traps. However, do not underestimate the power of fresh eyes either – excluding young, visionary and innovative titans is just as bad as missing senior knowledge.

Distribution of rights and responsibilities

If you have managed to finalize the number of founders, the next step is to share the obligations, responsibilities and the daily tasks among them, which is, again, not as easy as it seems. Most startuppers start their business with their friends and find it unnecessary to set the rules down at the very beginning, since they are friends sitting in the same boat anyway. They could not be more mistaken.

What they never or just rarely do is to write a contract. We strongly recommend writing down all the roles, responsibilities, expectations, possible rewards, etc. Remember, contracts are written as friends, but may be interpreted as enemies! Things can go wrong, and if a friendship is broken by the stress of leading a startup and owning different views on some decisions to be made, this can still save you from suffering undesirable legal or financial consequences. Writing the base down makes the picture clear for all parties and eases daily life as well.

First of all, if tasks have no owners, they may just get lost in the daily rush, and crucial things such as paying the bills or replying to customers may be totally forgotten when all are focusing on finding out something extraordinary and showing something new and spectacular to the world. There should be an order, an organogram setting down the daily duties for everyone – sharing all the unwanted tasks as well.

In the case of more founders, in most of the cases there is an alpha – or at least should be one – even if they say they work democratically. This is not a bad thing however: there are cases when there should be a leader who decides, who takes the responsibility and leads the team towards the way they think is the right one. In an ideal case the team of founders chooses a leader, who has the final word, and form an idea-meritocracy, meaning that the ideas of all members are going to be listened to, and the leader makes the decisions considering all the input and opinions received. This looks like an ideal way to operate, but sadly this is not what the majority of startups do. Listening to everyone is not easy – and becomes harder with the number of parties growing. Many leaders either fall into the misconception of being smarter than anyone else and make the important decisions alone, while others try to consider everyone's sometimes contradicting opinions so much that they fail to decide in the end. This may be prevented only via conscious self-development and team building, which can diminish our bias and guide us towards the right direction even in a state of panic.

The unwanted role of the CEO

CEOs are not born; they are made. However, when you look at an ordinary company, especially a large organization with decades of history on the market, the CEO is usually the one who takes the initiative and has the ambition to become a leader. In our experience, most startups have a different type of CEO: a CEO who either stood up for the challenge that nobody from the founder team wanted, or the one who decided to take the worst part of the work to support the founding team.

As a company keeps growing, the mundane daily tasks of salary, taxes, hiring, firing, contracts, project management, customer relationship management become a big part of someone's daily job, and usually, this "someone" ends up becoming the CEO. Not because they wanted it, or fought for it. Simply because no one else really wanted to do it. Eventually, someone from the founding team will take over the managerial responsibilities, whether they like it or not. If this does not happen sooner or later, the ship has no captain – which is rarely the right way to success. Believe it or not, there are plenty of companies where the people running the business try to NOT TO HAVE the title of the CEO. We can see companies out there having no CEO on their websites or in their introductions. Co-founder, yes, CEO, no. This could mean an easy downfall.

A fundamental problem with managerial roles is that you don't have any distinct points where you can celebrate success, so anyone used to creating more tangible value each and every day will find that role less exciting. Operational issues just keep piling up, there is always another problem requiring a solution, and as no one raises their hand voluntarily, they just tend to land on your table. The crucial point is to acknowledge this situation and realize when you reach the pivot point and turn your ship to new and unknown waters. As the CEO, you are the top manager and the leader – at times, an impostor, as you might feel, distanced from all the daily jobs you liked, understood and were good at.

Find new goals

One of the first steps in the transition is to define and experience success differently. Determine some KPIs, maybe even just for yourself. Leadership is a tricky bag of tricks. It is tough to see the progress, as in most cases, it happens every day in tiny increments, like the anecdotal 0.1% each day. If you keep pounding, it will eventually add up to a substantial change. If you look at it after a week, it's still invisible. For a year with 200 working days, that will be 22% better performance. So imagine how minuscule the daily or weekly change is. This is why you need to set quarterly KPIs, yearly KPIs, and celebrations. Celebrate when you see something done differently.

Start working ON the company, not IN the company

The next step is to find yourself challenges not only working IN the company, but also ON the company. The pivot point is when you realize that growth comes by changing the vantage point. Your vantage point. Being a double agent may be sustainable for a while and might give you the right balance of being an efficient member of the team and doing the necessary evil of being a part-time manager, you will eventually burn out or get stuck at a certain point. Being a member of the team, while also managing it as a leader is not a solution that could work for long.

Working on the company helps grow it into a more sustainable, more resilient company; a company that can endure crises, such as pandemic, war, or the losing of some key personnel, as working on the company will eventually result in the company being more than just the sum of the building blocks. It will become an entity of its own, maybe even independent of the founders. Even if you do not realize it, your clients will. They will work with and trust your company and not the people (as individuals) first.

That's when you have a company. That's where another story begins. The growth story, the global story. The goal is to achieve a sense of fulfillment, a sense of "having a worthy life". As a leader, you can have a more significant role and a bigger impact on everyone's life. On the culture and values of the company and therefore even on the personal lives of your colleagues by providing a safe space, a special place to be.

Develop personally

Achieving all these things and becoming a true leader requires you to work on yourself as well. You do not get to this point by just making a decision. You have become a professional in your field in years. This development requires the same commitment to learning and improving your skills. It can be done, others have done it before you and there will be others walking down the same path after you finish your career.

Risk taking

There is another important factor, which is good to be discussed before engaging in more complicated tasks: not all the founders have the same level of risk-taking ability. Entrepreneurs are usually not risk averse, but in most of the cases engineers and financial people are. Neither end of the scale is good. Too high a level of risk taking may result in the project running to death, while being risk averse rarely brings growth and brilliant ideas.

The ideal case is when some of the founders are risk takers, and some are more safe players, which can result in a balance, staying somewhere in the middle, but a bit closer to risk taking to be able to progress. Somehow you need to be bold, without losing your rational mind. This could work well, when communicated, but if founders are not aware and ready to listen to an opinion resulting from one's higher or lower level of risk aversion, that could result in heated arguments and accusations of one or another taking the company in the wrong direction. Both risk-taking and risk averse members are needed, but they need to be able to communicate and accept each other's sometimes highly different views to be able to cooperate, which is worth a good talk before signing anything.

#7·3·2 Hiring for a HW startup

After you have successfully worked yourself through founding a startup, you will not have too much time to relax: soon you will need to look for team members. Growth is manageable within the founding team for a while, but sooner or later – if growth is on the right track – expansion will result in the core team not being able to handle everything on their own. And that is going to be the time you need to make similar decisions than at the time of determining the number of founders: how many people you need to hire and which skills are essential and needed at the stage you currently are. However, on top of it, there are other important aspects to consider, since hiring someone is a completely different story than teaming up with other founders for a common goal.

Knowledge or personality?

There is a common myth to avoid, summarized in a great article, The Myth of 20 years of Engineering Experience by Ákos Tolnai. One of his mentors, who had his own share of patents in telecommunications said: 'Hardware and engineering are quite different. To have 20 years of engineering experience, you need to have exactly 20 years of engineering work experience'. On the contrary, not knowing how software was developed 20 years ago will not hurt your skills to become the best software developer of nowadays.

Hardware is engineering. The mistakes you can make in hardware manufacturing are not published on the internet under GPL license. They are in the cortices of the specialists you will be working with. Molding, welding, waterproofing, adhesive technology, printing, packaging, and numerous other fields are special, unique sets of experiences, which you cannot replace with enthusiastic juniors. We have not met a single founder on their first hardware project, who would not ignore the advice above, but believe 'You can learn it from books, or the internet'. without questioning. But sooner or later it turns out that most founders have absolutely no idea what different skill sets they are going to need during the manufacturing and development of the whole package. If you don't know what you don't know...

Talent is another important aspect of finding the right person to be hired – especially in the case of juniors. It is impossible to give the one and only solution, as it does not exist. It strongly depends on the product, technologies, complexity, and many other factors, what kind of talents you are actually going to need. The main point is to remind yourself to always start with a deep analysis before you open a new vacancy for each and every role. Talent is a natural aptitude or skill in something; and you need to find the right sets to look for. Would you like to hire a manager for a certain role or rather someone, who is good at execution? Do you need someone with good interpersonal skills or strategic thinking? Is it a down-to-earth or a visionary employee, who could add more to the success in the position you would like to fill? Numerous questions to ask and analyze before even sharing the vacancy.

Once you have figured out the skill sets you are looking for, there is another important question to consider: how valuable is that skill for you? Even though there are skill sets that cannot be replaced by enthusiastic juniors, and there are talents, which may rocket your performance at an instant, you always need to consider the match of each person to the team too. Being an expert at a unique field does not make up for having a difficult personality or being unfriendly or rude to leaders or other team members. However important a skill set is, it is never worth keeping a person on the price of ruining a whole team.

When interviewing a person, you not only have to look for expertise, but also a matching personality. We cannot suggest the right combination here – it depends on your team and on your personal judgment to identify those personality traits required besides owning a certain set of professional skills. What we can suggest to you, however, is to be aware of what you are looking for: consciously monitor your team, identify the personality traits you value or find harmful and make a checklist of the musts, good-to-have characteristics and the red flags. Be prepared and evaluate each potential person weighing all the aspects of expertise and personal characteristics before making decisions too quickly.

Hiring methods

There are just a few exceptional cases, when talented people are standing in line to work for a startup, especially for a hardware startup. If you are this one startup, you can feel lucky. However, in case you are not the chosen one, who can filter the best of the best on the first day after making the application open, there are some crucial factors for you to consider.

The first aspect to think about is who does the hiring. You can do the whole process yourself, or outsource some parts, or the complete process to a headhunter company.

Since in a startup, the level of trust towards each of the team members needs to be top level, therefore I would not suggest starting with a totally outsourced hiring campaign. Later, when you are looking for a 10th engineer, it could be a solution, but it is a hard thing to define the criteria required for company culture fit and turn it into a brief for an HR person or company. What more, these services are costly, which most of the start-ups – especially in the early stage – cannot afford.

Some parts of the hiring process may be outsourced to save the time of the founders – who need to deal with a pile of other tasks as well –, such as the first filtering of the potential applicants or buying a database of contacts. These are the more standardizable parts, which may be automated, but this way you keep the personal interview to yourself to make sure you hire the right person, who fits not only professionally, but personally as well.

Firing decisions and methods — when to let go

There is a very wise quote: hire slow, fire fast. We have already given you some ideas about the hiring, now it is time to let it go. Believe me, sometimes the best thing you can do is to let employees move on. If you see it is not working, it makes no sense to push it on.

All right, but how do I know if it is not working, and how do I know if it is me or the startup, and not the employee who causes the real issue? Well, it is a heavy topic. I, personally, have and always had struggles with this topic too: now I know that I should have made firing decisions earlier in my startup too. What I can suggest to you is to analyze, evaluate, try to eliminate the personal prejudices, discuss with co-founders and team members and try to focus on the facts to be as objective as possible.

But what kind of reasons could lead to firing an employee? There may be numerous reasons for this decision to be made, but as a guidance here you can see the most important red flags. If you see one (or more) of these, you should seriously think about letting go of the person:

- Being toxic to the team
- Not being able to fulfill requirements and cannot be trained, or coached
- Not delivering the commitments agreed on
- Does something against the company

It is hard to see the traits before they happen, especially if the processes are not there or not transparent enough; and it is also hard to fire somebody if the expectations were not communicated clearly enough at the beginning. This is why it is crucial – as we have already emphasized – to set the roles, obligations and responsibilities as early as possible. This not only gives guidance to the people on what is expected and prohibited, but also gives you a basis for sanctions, when things are starting to turn bad.

You, as founder, manager, CEO of a startup have two main objectives: delivering to customers and keeping the best workforce. Believe us, it is better to fire, than keeping harmful people on the board. It is not good for the startup, nor for the team or the employee. Be clear, specific, transparent, and fast. Nobody needs a long torture, but they deseve the truth, as painless as possible.

#7·3·3 Leading and managing a hardware startup

While the main focus of this book is not on leadership, this topic cannot be skipped, as it is the cornerstone of a successful business. You are a very special member, the leader, responsible for the delivery machine. Your words, gestures, behavior and deeds must represent your company culture and serve your strategy and goals – but you also need to be there for your people and serve them. This duality is not a piece of cake to handle. Here we are going to focus not on the leadership theories and practices – hundreds of books discuss this topic and we are going to suggest a few too –, but on some core aspects, which we think you should keep in mind as a leader and which could make your daily life easier.

Finding the right priorities

All the things you do and how you do them has to serve the startup at first. Secondary can be the team, you and anybody else. This sounds harsh at the beginning, but soon you will understand the point. Let's break this down to details!

You chose to serve a bigger goal. Bigger that one single human can achieve. The only way to do this is to give everything you have, find other people, who feel the same and make it happen. 'If you have dreams big enough, you don't need a crisis' – I heard that phrase from Paul Chek in a very unrelated topic, but the context does not take anything away from the meaning. It says that you need to work hard and keep your productivity at its peak, and so do your teammates'. This means not only cognitive, but also mental, emotional, and physical fitness. You cannot serve the greater good when you are exhausted and one step away from insanity. Do not sit on five horses at the same time! Focus on the goal and the steps you need to take to achieve it!

Being able to do this requires sacrifices. You need to prioritize, and probably forgo certain things for a while; as being a startupper normally does not mean having an endless amount of free time and money for holidays and parties – sometimes not even enough time for your family. Do not drive yourself insane or cut relationships with all the loved ones, but try to keep a healthy focus on the goal ahead.

Setting the priorities right is important when making startup-related decisions as well. The first should always be the goal of the project, second the team who makes the plan happen. If you need to hire a new person, as a new skill is needed, do not be afraid to make this step! If you have to let go of certain people for the sake of the team and the project, do it! There will not be any perfect decisions, but if you have clear goals and planned consciously before, you will be able to see the steps that serve the future of the startup the best. To enhance this, make a support system that serves and supports the maximum output and always prioritize the tasks and decisions that add the most to achieving the goal. Lead the team in this spirit all the way!

Attitude of the leader

There are some behavior traits that are hard to change or control, just as there are some physical appearances, which you have to accept. There is no description of a perfect leader, and probably all the leaders in the world have slightly different sets of characteristics (in spite of having common attributes too). This again is a really complex topic discussed in hundreds of books, but here we are going to highlight one very important thing: attitude.

We have already discussed the importance of awareness, approach and actions in Chapter #3, explaining how much personal behavior can influence the life of a startup – especially if it is that of the leader. This is why the most important thing you need to get right is to control your attitude and change it, if necessary. Attitude is every single step you are doing, every single word you say or write, every single action you take. It has an effect on your people, your team, your operations, your partners

– literally everything, since these are all connected: the startup needs to move like one unit, one system, one organism. Culture should be the heartbeat that dictates the rhythm and it is going to be you, who form it. You need to build a culture with a good attitude including trust, transparency, support, alignment and a good system.

Which attitude can make a startup fail?

- **Being too soft**
  Personally, I did this and the startup failed. I could not hold my team accountable, I trusted them more than the level of authority they could handle. The project was sexy, but not their own, so they did not feel the responsibility I felt, and not being aware of this was clearly my fault. My attitude was too friendly and I did not state my expectations and performance standards clearly enough. Being kind and understanding should have its limits, and I have learnt this the hard way. No matter how nice people they are, they are not your family, but employees and team members, who have a job to do.

- **Being too hard**
  Being an a**hole is not the best strategy either. Being a dictator is the way to high fluctuation and burnout of the team members. Often these managers are also control freaks, micromanaging their people till the tiniest detail, since they need the feeling of power on every level. This is just as harmful as not supervising the team enough, but this way you lose not only the space for personal thoughts and creativity, but also deprive people of authority and the feeling of being trusted.

Most of the managers represent one of the two ends of the scale. One of them is the boss with the stone cold heart, hitting every milestone, but more often than not, the salaries of the employees are spent on a variety of drugs and alcohol to help them suffice before they ultimately burn out and quit. The other extreme is the good cop surrounding himself with a team like a family; with the unfortunate matter of having no processes in place to hold the team or himself accountable, thus being unable to hit goals or propagate real growth. Both ends are unacceptable for a startup, even though they can (sadly) work in a big company with financial stability, where changing the course takes years and fluctuation is not such a big issue.

Long story short, you have to be the leader of special forces, keeping your team dedicated, motivated and willing to risk everything for the BHAG (Big Hairy Audacious Goal*) without pushing them beyond the limit and utilizing their last drops of energy too. Supervise them, be the leader, not just a random member of the team, but do not drain their individuality and motivation. This is easier said than done; especially as every team and individual is different, requiring various levels of supervision. Just like in many cases before, we cannot give you the secret recipe on how to do it, but this is where emotional intelligence becomes crucial. You as a leader need to learn how to lead your diverse and valuable team, considering individual needs and abilities, but still, setting the same set of expectations to avoid the feeling of inequality.

---

* (A Big Hairy Audacious Goal is a clear and compelling target for an organization to strive for. The term was coined in the book "Built to Last: Successful Habits of Visionary Companies" by Jim Collins and Jerry Porras.; source: Investopedia)

Personal development

It is a long journey to develop yourself to be a good leader and manager. Doing it in a startup is the harder path. As a founder, you need to deal with other founders as well, not just the team, which can bring a whole lot of unexpected problems. The best you can do is to try to prepare for any kind of situation and train yourself to be able to make the best out of them. But how can you achieve this?

In most cases you would be advised to participate in different kinds of training sessions and workshops, which, of course, as a founder of an emerging startup you probably cannot afford. However, this does not mean that you will be deprived of this knowledge! Nowadays, if you are proactive enough, you can gather a huge amount of knowledge on your own too. Books, YouTube and TEDx videos and podcasts are endless sources of knowledge if you take the time and effort to find the ones you need and make your way through them. Searching is hard and processing the huge amount of knowledge is even harder, so here we provide you with a starter pack of useful books you can read to develop as a leader.

The Making of a Manager: What to Do When Everyone Looks to You (Julie Zhou)
Practical advice, effective teamwork, timetables. Situations every manager has to, or will face.

Leadership Is Language: The Hidden Power of What You Say and What You Don't (L. David Marquet)
To us, it is the ultimate guidance on how to apply the essential books and insights of the last decade: candor communication,

growth mindset, lean startup, and even more. It's extremely practical. Conversations, questions, techniques, words to use, and to avoid, why to avoid specific phrases.

The Five Dysfunctions of a Team: A Leadership Fable (PAtrick Lencioni)

The author has made a five-step model, highlighting the critical sources of problems in a team. It offers a nice handle to show whether a team is functioning properly. A must-read for agile teams.

Mindset: The New Psychology of Success (Carol S. Dweck)

Our genes influence our intelligence and talents, but these qualities are not fixed at birth. People with a fixed mindset think intelligence is static: either you are smart, or you are not. People with a growth mindset believe intelligence can be developed. This book helps you understand the two perspectives, shows you why you should rather want to have a growth mindset, and gives you tools to avoid fixed mindset.

Radical Candor: Be a Kick-Ass Boss Without Losing Your Humanity (Kim Scott)

Innovation requires being open to feedback – fast and direct feedback, even in the most stressful situations. Radical candor demonstrates how to do that and how it can help in creating the right feedback culture.

Communication styles

A crucial trait of a leader is to be able to communicate – formally and informally, internally and externally, with partners, suppliers, competitors, the authorities, certification bodies... and literally anyone the startup is interacting with. This requires not only the right set of priorities, attitude and knowledge, but also high level communication skills, to be able to negotiate, manage conflicts, express expectations, praise and assert interests.

A communication method is said to be good, when it is free from prejudices and judgment, but expresses needs clearly. This is when we talk about assertive communication, which is, again, easier said than done. People often fall into the mistake of communicating in a passive or aggressive way, which is usually strongly linked to the attitude of a leader being too soft or too hard. Equally to the extremes in attitude, here we may observe two extremes of a scale as well.

Passive communicators tend to bow to the will of others, accepting their views and requests, often without expressing their own preferences. This, as a leader is a total no-go, therefore less frequently seen; as expressing expectations and being able to stand up for one's own views is a must if we would like to lead anyone or anything. If a leader of a startup is a passive communicator, we do not think the company can last for long. We need warriors here!

What we see way more often among leaders is the aggressive communication method, when one tries to rule the communication process and force their own views and ideas on others, sometimes even without listening to them. This, just like a leader being too hard on the employees, is one of the best ways to ruin motivation, creativity and cooperativity.

Assertive communication represents the golden mean between the two extremes: listening to and considering what other people have to say, reflecting on it, but expressing our own needs clearly as well. A leader good in communication is able to clarify the expectations towards an employee clearly and with respect, also considering their personal abilities and needs. This is something you can read about, something you can consciously train and improve even in a very short time.

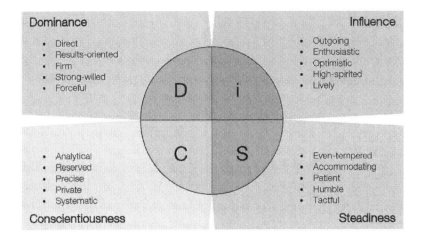

However, even if you think you can communicate in the right – assertive – way, it is still not going to solve all your communication issues. Talking about communication styles, we need to mention the DISC model. This model describes four main behavioral styles, as you can see on the picture below – since people are not the same; and even though there are some general principles you may apply, they are still diverse, having different personalities, experiences and needs, which you need to consider. Why do we address the DISC model here? Because the DISC type of the person tells you how to communicate with them from informal talks to task delegation. A 'D' person needs clear targets and goals, an 'I' person needs cheering and sublime thoughts, an S person needs slower communication, peace and understanding, while a 'C' person needs data the most.

More on that in the books of Thomas Erikson, who wrote the famous 'The Surrounded by Idiots' series, in which he 'shares a groundbreaking new method of understanding the people around you that will change how you interact with everyone from your coworkers to your spouse' (as the book description on Goodreads says).

How to communicate, technically

Besides the communication styles in general, it is worth saying a couple of words about technical solutions for communication as well. We know that having 6 hours of meetings a day is not feasible, since we also have other things to do, but nor is communicating in emails exclusively, as we need to dedicate time to discuss things as well. Neither of the extreme solutions are efficient and we cannot completely replace one with the other. But what is efficient? Again, you need to find the best solution for yourself, but we can give some handrails, some general advice, which may make your life easier.

The first things you need to think through are what, how, why, and to whom you are communicating, and what could be the most efficient way of doing that. Delegating tasks, asking for reports, brainstorming, daily status meetings, weekly development meetings, and other occasions all need different tools and methods. Not all meetings need to be in-person, and not every session requires the participants to use their laptops or phones. Some meetings may be held online, while others need to happen in person in any case.

Make a plan about the different occasions for communication: goals, methods, tools, frequency, and participants for every single case. Use written communication, when enough and appropriate, and organize online or in-person meetings, when necessary. Make a framework for online and in-person meetings including important details, such as who is leading a meeting, who documents it, and how the information is going to be shared. E-mail is a useful and semi-official way to communicate, but within the company this could be sometimes too small and inefficient, so there should also be a way of fast communication, e.g. a company Slack channel, or chat, where the important information may be shared quickly and efficiently.

The best way to formalize information exchange within the company is to write down the policy of communication, both written and verbal. This may sound embarrassing or unnecessary, but it really helps a lot when the team knows how to communicate, which channels to use for different purposes and where to find the information they need. Having a clear guidance on this may save you from misunderstandings and work hours to be wasted.

#7·3·4 Some other items related to People

- Hiring strategy [P]
  - Competencies
  - Hire for potential?
  - Company culture fit
- Boarding process [P]
  - Boarding experience [P]
  - New employee integration [P]
  - Employee experience [P]

- ▫ Training plan [P]
- ▫ Equipment: Laptop, phone, etc. [P]
- Contracts, e.g. vesting [P]
- Employee stock option ESO [P]
- Engineering team [P]
- Expectations [P]
- Learning organization [B, P]
  - ▫ Storming, Froming, Norming, Performing [P]
- Backoffice solutions [P]
  - ▫ Automation [P]
- Roles [P]
- Responsibilities [P]
- Accountability [P]
- Traceability [P]
- Transparency [P]
- Delegation [P]
- Competencies [P]
- Voice of employee [P]
- Keeping up momentum [P]
- Focus on priorities [P]
- Framework
  - ▫ Agile [P]
  - ▫ Scrum [P]
  - ▫ PM [P]
- Commitments [P]
- Coaching + stretching [P]
- Radical truth and transparency [P]

#7·4 Finances

Everything has a price and a cost in life – and so do the items in every phase of the business. The product is meant to be sold, employees are meant to be paid and so are the suppliers. Incomes should cover the costs and profit needs to be enough for the management and for the investors, if any. To be able to manage and keep track of all these things and make ends meet, you need to have a realistic, accurate and up-to-date financial plan including all the important details, even the tiniest ones. It is not enough to make a good-looking financial plan at the beginning, you need to groom, refresh, and rethink it from time to time – since no financial plan survives the first encounter with the customer and I know nobody, who has ever heard of a financial plan that had never been changed.

As a startup, you need to be flexible, but finance and finance experts are not famous for their flexibility. In every country there are laws and regulations that need to be considered. This 'extra' administration and workload seems to be excess effort making no sense and being against you, but they are not. If you build your company accordingly from the first day on, it will help you stay transparent, which is also preferred by the investors, and at the time of exit.

Just like in the case of the other layers, here we are going to discuss the items from the finance layer we regarded as important and worth mentioning separately.

#7·4·1 Cash(flow)

You may have a certain amount of money in the bank, but your burn-rate can increase with the investments, sourcing, and salaries, as you saw in business and technology. With every month of delay to the initial plan, you will risk the survival of the start-up, as you need to pay the bills, the salaries, and the additional costs of the delay. Different payment terms in your sales and supply chain can also cause problems in cases. When you have already paid for the parts and materials, assembled the parts, sold the finished goods, and the customer is only going to pay in two months time, many startups face serious issues. This, however, is a normal practice in the B2B sector, which startuppers need to be aware of, and have to try to make sure the company survives such delays. Unexpected expenses may occur anytime as well, due to changes in material prices, exchange rates, legal requirements, fines incurred by compliance issues – or literally anything that can happen in such a volatile business environment. Ensuring the financial resources to be able to operate – even in case of problems – is essential to prevent shutting down after the first bunch of issues occur.

#7·4·2 (Bank) Guarantee

As startups are new financial entities, risk averse companies are often skeptical towards them, therefore they seek for some guarantee – any kind of guarantee of getting their loss covered in case the startup goes bankrupt. This is more a demand than a wish from their side. They would like to work with you, but they do not want to share your risk. This results in a certain level of risk-reward asymmetry, but it is – until a certain point – understandable.

There is a chance, you will need to put a huge amount of money on the table for the materials, sometimes for the whole year's amount, especially for the long-lead-time components, or you need to give everything as procured. This reduces the obsolete risk basically to zero on their side, so they play safe. Besides this discriminatory treatment, they often price the goods and services more expensive, to cover the extra effort and extra support they give. Sweet, isn't it?

However, it is still them you need to work with and however cruel they sound, their actions are still defendable from their risk averse and more rigid perspective. Guarantees can improve their trust towards your company, which can result in fruitful future relationships, so accepting their terms to an extent can be beneficial for your company – but be careful, not to take the lead too much!

#7·4·3 Investment

As a HW startup investments may reach the skies soon enough, As every other company, you will probably invest in production equipment as well, no matter if you choose in-house or outsourced production. In-house means it is you who is paying for everything including planning and setting up the production plant and equipping it to your needs, followed by the continuous maintenance costs, which, as we have discussed before, is rarely feasible for a startup at the beginning of its journey.

But even if you choose outsourcing as a production model, there are some investments to be made in the equipment for production. It is the supplier, who sets up the production equipment in their own plant, but they do it for your request, which needs to be rewarded sooner or later, since, of course, your interest would be the dedicated equipment to be used only for your project if you pay for it to your suppliers. There are basically two options. Either you buy it (with a purchase order, or you buy it directly and give it to the supplier) or you hide the costs into the piece-price. E.g. the investment is 10 000 € and you say, you will pay 2€ more for every 5 000 pieces. Both options are applied often, and the most important deciding factors are going to be your financial opportunities. The only important thing is – just like in the case of any investment – to weigh the costs and benefits of each option and have a clear financial plan – this can save you from a lot of unwanted surprises.

#7·4·3 Sublayers you need to take in consideration

- Starting a startup
  - Financial plan
  - Capital need [F]
  - Investor or no investor
  - Right investor [F]
  - Exit strategy [F]
- Planning
  - Financial plan (reviews)
  - Money and pivots left [F]
  - Financial periods Vs development of the company

- Operation
  - Costs
    - Cost structure [F]
    - Investments [B, T, F]
    - One-time costs [B, T, F]
    - Budgeting
  - Revenue
    - Product(s)
    - Service(s)
    - Recurring revenue
    - Margin
    - Pricing model
  - Cashflow cycle
    - Cashflow cycle compared to business partners
  - Used currencies
    - Hedging
    - Bank accounts
  - Financial stability
  - Cashburn rate [F]
    - of the competitors, customers and supply chain
  - VAT, taxes, customs [F]
  - Risk mitigation
    - Bank guarantee towards business partners

#8 Roadmap

"Victorious warriors win first and then go to war, while de-
feated warriors go to war first and then seek to win."

Sun Tzu, The Art of War

Let this be your mantra. Without knowing what you need to do, without proper planning of the journey, the surprises that can occur could hit you as hard as a concrete wall.

By the time you are reading this chapter of the book, you already understand the real complexity of hardware startups and have a general overview of the lean startup method, our suggested updates, and other useful tools. The next step is to combine all this into a functioning system and create your own roadmap.

In the following we will give you some hints to help you find the smallest interpretable steps of your own roadmap. To achieve this, you can apply two basic approaches: one of them is the reverse engineering of the product and production, and the second is the bottom-up planning, where you build the phases up step by step, starting from the idea, going towards production start and beyond. Both methods make sense. The main question of the first one is 'What do I need to achieve that?' and for the second one, it is 'What should I do next?' We will give you a frame, which you can use for both roadmap-building methods.

Priorities of the layers

It can be an interesting question, which layer you should base and build your startup on. The answer is: it depends. This may not help at the moment at all, but in reality, it is better than choosing one layer and carving the base in stone – which can be misleading, since priorities can –, and will – change in every stage of the lifecycle of the startup, the product, and the business. The dominating layer, which you consider as prio one is on the other hand a strategic question, heavily influenced by the background of the founders. You can choose Technology, Business, or People as the foundation of the project, but there is no ultimate best choice.

Considering the phases of the startup, at first, you need to be a learning organization and besides focusing on the business aspects, of course, People layer should always be there, providing a stable base for everything (yet, the focus often shifts from this area to more acute problems). In the development phase you focus both on Business and Technology, while coming to production, you focus more on Technology, and more and more on Finance topics as well.

People	Business	Technology	Finance
The prio at first is the People domain. You need a team hungry to learn	Second you need to set Business in prio to find out customer needs and understand the deepest motivation	If you know what the market will, you need to turn it into specification, documentation, prototype, product and finished good ready to send out. Of course some back and forth changes between Business and tech will happen.	From the first product produced you need to turn 100% corporate and let the numbers say what to do.

None of us sees the future, so it is impossible to write the complete project plan with a proper scheduling of resources, broken down to days. It is unrealistic. Things are moving and changing, especially after every bigger change in the startup while it is growing up to become a big company. You cannot forget this fact, while planning your roadmap. To give you a better insight into the individual phases, we will now introduce what the different phases are like, and how you can plan your own roadmap considering them. What we regard as realistic at this stage is to create a roadmap containing the key milestones, relying on a vision-based strategy of yours. It might change by the time passing, as it is influenced by numerous factors, but still, it can give you guidance on where you are on your path and which way you should be heading.

On your roadmap there will be three kinds of tasks and achievements you can face. These may be

- Phase specific
- Overarching
- Non-bound

Phase specific tasks and achievements are tasks, which provide the basis of that phase. A good example of this may be design freeze, the ending point of the design phase, when no changes to the design are going to be made anymore, and your design is finalized. This achievement is yours, when the design of the product is mature enough to be feasible, production is also manageable and the functions and the look are also validated.

Overarching topics are more general, you cannot fix them to a certain point, as they are going to be important in multiple phases. The perfect example is validation. Validation is a big topic, and you are going to need it from time to time; practically speaking: ALWAYS.

Non-bound tasks and achievements are even more general, and in most cases related to daily operation, such as topics related to the people layer and the general functioning of your team. Being non-bound, however, does not mean you do not have to deal with them. On the contrary! Ignoring these tasks may result in the downfall of your startup even in spite of the product being good and you performing well in the other layers.

Please note: It is important to understand that every road-map is based on a product lifecycle. Every big update basically creates another product (version 2.0), and not a version 1.1.0.1. Plan accordingly!

In the following we are going to cover the same phases and milestones we have discussed so far:

- Idea phase
- Development phase
- Preparation for production phase
- SOP to SOS phase
- Product lifetime on market phase
- EOL phase

You can, of course, have more and/or different milestones based on your business and your product; the only important thing is to define your own milestones and their criteria according to your project. The most crucial things to determine are the starting point, the goal, the knockout and acceptance criteria, and the quality gates.

For each of the four phases there are also special traps you should avoid and tricks and tips that can save you money, time or the life of your project. Let's see them one by one!

#8·1 Idea phase

In this phase you have something in your mind. Something unclear, but you have a good feeling about it. You start to think more and more about it, and tell it to your friends, colleagues, and family. They ask 'dumb' questions, and you easily get upset. Why are you upset? You either think the answer is obvious – which is apparently not – or you do not know the answer either. It is totally fine not to know all the answers, but you will need to have them sooner or later. You need to take the time and other resources to find them, so the goal of this phase is going to be to find the right answers to the right questions in a resource-effective way.

The best way to find good answers is finding other people, who are able to ask more and better questions, or have the knowledge to answer some of the questions you probably cannot. This is why the People layer should be the one you start with. When you already have (some of) the people you need, you start working on the idea itself and the validation of it, therefore the Business layer is going to be activated.

At the end of this phase you would like to find answers to the following questions, and reach the following goals:

- Understand the problem
- Understand why the solution is the solution
- Understand the decision making process of the customer
- Understand the market
- Have a list of what you know, what you do not know and what you need to know
- Know whom you need on the board for success
- See the big picture and the complexity
- Have a business plan
- Have a realistic financial plan with all the main factors included
- Have a realistic timeline for the project
- Know what the product should be like, so you can move on to the development phase

The deadliest trap of all in this phase is to make false assumptions. The bold vision of your dream can make you more confident than you should be. You think you know perfectly well what your future customers will think, which may be true, but in most cases it is not. Try to let go of your biases and look deep into the issue to make sure you see what you are supposed to see and not what you would like to!

#8·2 Development phase

The team is ready to start the product – and later the production – development. The first step here is to turn the idea into a technical specification including as much of the fine details as possible. Based on that, prototypes are going to be built, and, in the end a finalized product will be born.

In this phase the Technology layer will dominate, directly followed by the Business layer, and supported by the People layer, as the team grows. The Technology and the Business layer will work closely together to validate all the changes on the market, develop a good product, keeping the business model alive. People are going to be needed, so the founders' team is not the only one working on the project anymore. Hiring and outsourcing processes are going to start, while you also need to keep your focus on the product, since it is taking its final form just now.

Typical problems are waiting in the way of the product to be perfect, which you need to overcome to be able to start preparing for production. You need to learn what a mature enough design means, and what the things are that can still be changed later without too significant effects on cost or work need. Being market ready with the product is not the same here, as at SW startups. You need a 100% functioning design, which can be manufactured and also assembled; and only some minor things, e.g. packaging, some extra ribs on the plastic parts, color changes are those that can be done later.

At the end of this phase you would like to find answers to the following questions, and reach the following goals:
- Have a design freeze
  - You have considered all the important manufacturing aspect
  - Specifications are ready and available

- Made x number of prototypes
  - You have got better and better results every time
- Customers still love the product – or love even more than before
- The manufacturing model has been decided
- The manufacturing process is planned

Do not forget: HW production is not something you can change from one day to another! Hard, we know, but try to specify everything as much as possible and do not change things over and over again! IF you would like to enter the next phase, you need to stop and make the final decision: 'yes, this is what we are going on with!'.

#8·3 Preparation for production phase

In this phase the work continues, the goal is to have a product ready for production. This phase is about all kinds of engineering, therefore mainly about Technology – and People, since it is them who do the engineering after all. SW and HW development, process, quality, logistic, packaging, validation, testing, and sales engineers work together to run the production and produce hundreds and thousands of perfect quality products. To make it even more complicated, literally everything can be a trap here: details should be as fine and exact as possible, and the tiniest difference in any of them may ruin the whole process, making you have to start everything all over again. The tiny details highlighted in the Technology layer all matter here, documentation, change management and certifications are all important elements, which cannot be overlooked.

Now let's see what it actually takes to reach the point production. Last step: Green light, production can start. What do we need for that? Let's reverse engineer the process!

- We know what and how we need to produce
  - Forecast is available → at this point it can be based on planned demand or preorders
  - Assembly and other work instructions are available
  - Quality checklists are there
  - People are trained
- Production line is available
  - Development of the line is complete
  - Equipment, tools, and fixtures are ready for use
  - Materials are available, in labeled holders
  - Workplaces are ergonomic and help the workers
  - Work environment is healthy: good air quality, light and cleanliness
- Assembly process is lean and balanced
- All the engineering series went well, there are no open tasks
  - 0 series went well → trial production with bigger quantity, and the involvement of people, who will do that later
  - Production line and process is robust → Run&Rate or similar was done, which is a proof of the capability of the process
  - Machines and testers are robust → Need to be validated! Dummy products with planned failure mode are also welcome.
  - Product can be assembled without any issues
  - Material flow is good
  - Tact time is near to planned

- Materials on stock (long term supply is also there) → Long term material availability has to be checked regularly
- Production equipment is reliable → enough spare parts are also available
- Workers are trained
- Warehouse is ready to receive the finished goods
- Distribution channels are prepared, the marketing campaign launched
- How do we know if we have left this stage? → Please see the first bullet point!

This phase is the main rehearsal of the continuously running play. You need to fight till the last man standing to achieve the point when the production can start without major compromises. There is no way you could skip this phase – this is the foundation of all the next steps!

#8·4 SOP to SOD phase

As Murphy's law states 'If something can go wrong, it will'. Most of the team members may have heard that before this phase too, but not as often as in this period: the time span from the start of the production to the start of delivery. This is the period with the most traps; and what was true during the preparation for production is even more enhanced to be true here.

SOD is the time when we can talk about regular delivery, not just the first one. This is definitely not the time to sit back and enjoy everything running smoothly without any issues. On the contrary: you still need to be focused on starting the production, but also need to keep it running, which is definitely a focus on the Technology layer, but the whole support team has to be there to react in time in case any problem appears, which is why People is still a highly important factor.

When the production has already started, the target is to have a controlled learning curve of production efficiency without any problems in quality, or quantity. The workers will learn how to assemble the product, acquire all the steps, and know where the materials are on the line. It is unnecessary stress to demand 100% output from the first day on. You need to support them by providing them with knowledge, a sufficient amount of materials, engineers to solve issues, and an open ear for their experience and suggestions.

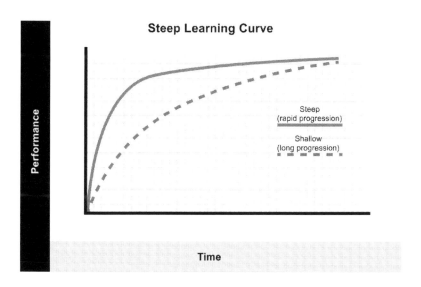

How do you know if you are there and when you can leave this stage?

- The market reacts well on the product
- Success metrics are good or promising
- The conditions are ready for real distribution to start
- Learning curve is visible and existing
    - Workers are more confident day by day
    - Production output grows
- Capacity is built-up → you can serve customers
    - Production capacity exceeds the demand
    - Logistic capacity exceeds the demand
- Start of delivery happens

This phase is all about learning, improving and developing to be able to produce faster, better, with less scrap and less mistakes, so this is also the phase where most of the issues arise. Stay strong and do not give up! Learning is hard, but you will see the benefits!

#8·5 Product lifetime on market phase

This phase starts with SOD (start of delivery). This phase is the one, where the company focuses on the fulfillment of the orders, the market gets filled with the product, and the long hours of development and planning finally pay off. The Finance layer is dominating here, as most of the People, Technology and Business issues have been settled by now, and at this point the startup already operates with all the functions of a production company. This is – hopefully – by far the longest period of the company, even though the previous phases must have seemed to be infinitely long.

Even though it seems, this is not the phase of setback and relaxation. Different challenges are waiting for you, such as storing goods, managing logistics, organizing service and maintenance, and keeping the production running, aligned with the (forecasted) demand on the market and grooming of the sales pipeline and marketing campaigns. You need to build stock, either in your warehouse, or in the warehouse of your distributors. This stock has to be there in time and delivered to the customers in good quality, and in case of quality issues, you need to react quickly and accurately.

All of these are both traps and opportunities, at the same time. If you treat the right, they can bring you progress, but if something is missing, the whole castle may burn down.

How do you know if you are there?

- The product is being sold on the markets
  - Production, sales, and delivery started
  - Sales performance is measured and tracked
  - All the early stage quality issues are solved
  - Customers are happy
  - After innovators and early adopters, the majority is also buying the product

When do you have to leave this stage?

- Sales drop significantly

When the sales numbers are decreasing, hopefully your next product is already near to launch. It can be an organic product lifecycle, but you can also apply an artificial pressure to push newer and newer products and product lines to the market, like mobile phone manufacturers are doing. Lifecycles may be shorter or longer depending on numerous factors, but the most important thing is to never stop working! Products will come and go, but if you would like to stay on the market, you always need to remain active and alert!

#8·6 EOL phase

You may think, this phase is so far away that it does not make any sense to even mention it. However, it is an important part of the product life cycle, and nowadays it gets more and more focus with the goal of zero waste product life cycles.

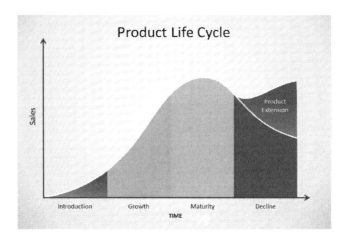

Many think that if something is over, then it is over and you just have to let it go. But what about the people? What about the machines, the production lines and all the things set up just for your product to reach the market? Luckier is the case when by the end of the lifetime the product you are dealing with is not the only one of your company, therefore the end of its distribution does not mean you need to shut down completely.

However, in either case, it is not so simple as just stopping production and starting something else. First of all, People need to be considered: you need to communicate about the future, tell them about the options and their roles in them. Should they leave and look for another job or can they stay? If they stay, do they have to learn new things and engage in different tasks, or can they have similar jobs as before? Just like in the beginning, the People layer should be the basis of the decisions made and the actions taken. Business and Financial sides are equally important at this point. You need to communicate with your contract manufacturers, suppliers and business partners about the future, end current transactions and settle open financial issues. Technology is not going to be in the focus anymore – except if you decide on trying your luck with some product variants –, since production is about to end,

How do you know if you are in this stage?

- Sales drop continuously and the signs of the decline phase are visible

What are the actions you should take to handle the situation the best?

- Make sure the phase out of the product is controlled, communicated well, as for the old product, so the new successor!

- Have a communicated plan for customer care after the product is not available on the market anymore! Customers like when they feel the care of the companies.

Remember, this is not just the end of a product, but also a new beginning, with improved products, processes, and customer experience!

#8·7 The carrier matrix — Timing

"What can happen, will happen" is a quote by Dr. Manhattan in the movie Watchmen, which fits here perfectly.

Timing is really like a web, a carrier matrix of everything. There is an opportunity to make a great product. You may perceive this as an opportunity window which is very limited. The project timing is set at initial planning, and you try not to deviate from it. You feel the time pressure harder and harder every day. But as it usually happens, not everything goes as planned.

Rule Nr. 1: It takes longer. Much longer
You may think everybody works as agile as you do. Anyway, you are also just at the beginning. You will realize soon enough that communication takes longer, time zone differences give at least 1 extra day for answers, optimization loops take longer, lead times will be worse than you expect, and you will face more changes and pivots than you think. It will put a hell of an amount of stress on your team and on the manufacturer; and, believe me, they are unlikely to take the responsibility for your junior

engineers' mistakes made due to their lack of experience and knowledge.

Rule Nr. 2: Where you can lose time, you will
Sadly, this results from rule Nr. 1. You need to plan with it, to keep it in your mind all the time. Minor mistakes will be the cornerstone of the project. It is part of it. Keep going!
Resilience is the key.

Optimistic or realistic
There are two ways of handling the timing plan: optimistic or realistic. Both have their benefits and disadvantages too. The reason behind that is the perception of time and the time pressure.

The optimistic way puts more pressure on the team, it is a constant sprint. Everybody knows it is often not realistic, there is no time calculated for iterations. Even if Elon Musk or Steve Jobs is your chief of engineering, it is sometimes impossible to reduce the time. A good example for that is the capacity of your suppliers. It is a misbelief to think they are sitting there, doing nothing and waiting for your order to be fulfilled.

The realistic one on the other hand has too much buffer and the latency will be even more, as all the optimization is calculated. In the beginning you will lose time, then, at the end the time pressure will be so high, that mistakes will be followed by mistakes.

Your team will burn out with the first one and become too lazy with the second one. The truth is in the middle.

#8·8 Practical insights to the creation of your roadmap

Now that you have got an overview on everything, it is time you build your own roadmap! Write all the important tasks, milestones, obstacles, or problems to solve on a sticky note or insert them into a text box, draw a timeline, and put everything on it...

...and what you get is a nightmare of every sane person:

It is even worse if you can zoom in and see all the small blocks. As you can see, this is a complex game. Fortunately every complexity can be divided into small pieces you can manage to address. You need to do the same here. What you need to master is zoom in and zoom out. It is like breathing. Take new information as you inhale, and integrate it to the whole picture as you exhale.

You are the leader, the captain, the chief, the general, the boss. You are standing on the highest point of the field to have the overview. First, you need to zoom out to see the whole picture. Here you need the awareness mentioned in #3. This is the total overview of what you need to know, broken down to the smallest detail.

The next step is zooming in to a particular problem or task. First you isolate it to understand, and then you slowly zoom out to reintegrate it to the whole picture and to understand how it is connected to other roadmap items.

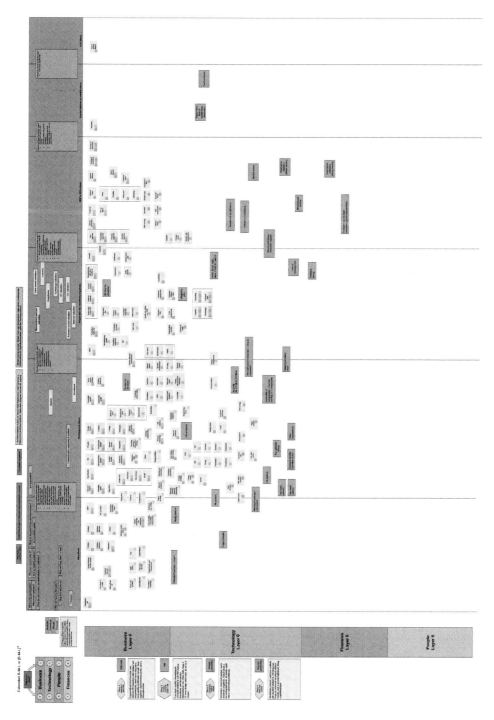

(This is an actual dummy roadmap with almost all the relevant items.)

Let's pick a random roadmap item:

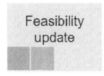

Feasibility [B, T] study is an important part of the product development process from an engineering point of view. If we zoom in, we see a form to fill with a purpose. When zooming out, we understand how it is connected to Business and Technology topics, we can connect it to the other items related, and change everything accordingly.

If there are items, which are different entities, but strongly related, you can also group them on the roadmap for a better understanding. Let's see another example:

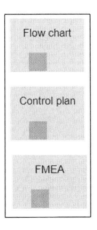

The flow chart describes the process, the control plan collects the parameters you can and should measure, and the FMEA (both design and product) shows what can go wrong, how big of a problem it is, and helps you make corrective actions. If you group them, you can see everything together.

Keep a living set of documents where you store historical data and progress simultaneously. The most important documents among these are the feasibility study and the Flow Chart-Control Plan-FMEA trio we mentioned above, but also a risk analysis, a vision board, a roadmap, a feature list, and the validation documents. Keep them available for the team, keep them transparent and regularly updated! These help you to stay on track.

Involve the whole team in planning and updating your roadmap. By this you keep the people involved, motivated, and provide them with the feeling of responsibility. Seeing the whole picture is important for many. I used to make the mistake of delegating tasks without telling people how it is going to contribute to the whole project. I lost the interest of many team members because of feeling excluded.

A good roadmap can be one of the most important alignment tools for your journey. After we have discussed this, we have nothing else to do but to summarize everything we have collected here.

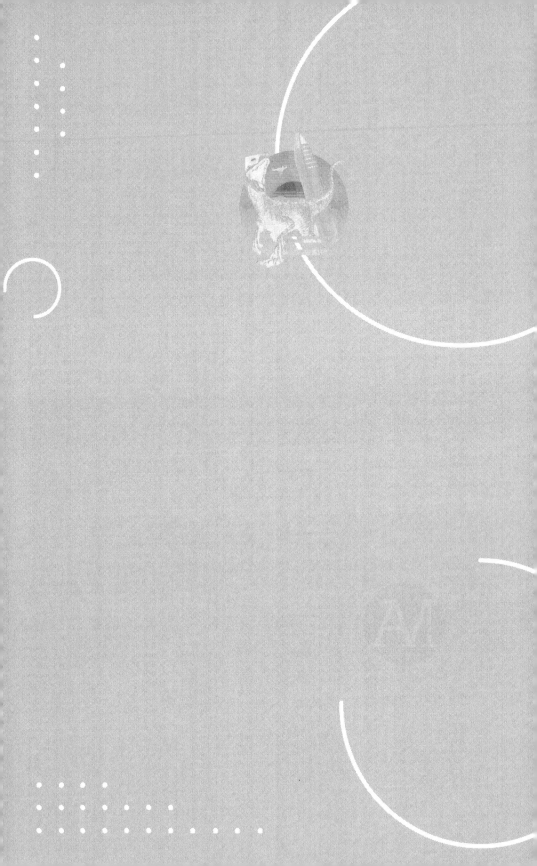

#9 Summary

As you can see, hardware is really hard, but the battle is not in every case a lost one. It is rather complex than difficult. The individual items and tasks are manageable, it is their quantity that makes the whole picture chaotic. The solution is planning and replanning frequently on many levels, making things transparent and visible, and this alignment is going to be the thing giving you and the team the Northern Star of the project.

The success of a HW startup depends on how well you can coordinate the dance of the layers. They are constantly changing their order, priority, and weight during the phases. There is always a dominating one, but you cannot skip the other three either. It is hard not to get lost in the depth of the layers. The complexity of the Technology layers needs to be compensated with competences and experience. For the other layers, rational thinking, modeling, and planning are almost enough.

It helps a lot if you find a good mentor, other startups who went through a similar journey even if they failed, or get mentored by a big company. Soon big companies will realize this and activate themselves more and more. On the other end of the industrial company size spectrum, the Renaissance of small engineering offices is also near. They could be the key to the above-mentioned founder competency gap. Small, flexible teams you can "rent" and use as your own, like agile delivery teams in SW development.

If the necessary and sufficient brainpower is available, the base plan is ready, you need to be disciplined and focused enough to execute your Masterplan. Our framework will be a faithful companion on that journey. Look for further resources and deepen your knowledge in these topics, e.g. hire an agile coach, scrum masters, product owners, and also traditional industry experts.

Start your journey, build great products! Your innovations are needed more than ever. We will be there to support you!

You can find our contact data in the about us section. We are happy to get feedback, read your stories and experience.

#10 What's next

After reading in this book you may ask, what the next move should be. Hopefully, we have initiated a process in your head to think, rethink, learn and relearn. This is an important part of the journey: learning, experiencing, experimenting. You have to grow with, or, if you can, even faster than your startup, otherwise soon enough you will not be able to lead it anymore.

Every source of information is useful if you develop your critical thinking and a healthy skepticism. Do not worry, it will develop naturally by the time passing and the experience you gain. Keep being thirsty for knowledge, both practical and theoretical! Keep listening, digesting, and utilizing new information! Always ask yourself: how can I use this? What is this going to teach me?

Learning in itself is not enough, whatsoever: after a while you reach your boundaries, and no matter how good of a learner you are, sooner or later you are going to need guidance too. This is when you need to find a mentor, a person you can look up to, someone who is able to support you, to guide you – and warn you if you are heading in the wrong direction.

Courses, coaching sessions and seminars could help a lot too, but for many of us – especially when working on a newborn startup – they are simply out of reach. If you have the opportunity to participate, do not miss it, but do not lose spirit if not! Here we are going to give some guidance on how to develop on your own. We list you some important sources of knowledge, which have helped us a lot – and could hopefully help you too.

However, there is one thing you should never forget: Spending too much time on learning and personal development instead of working on your startup is also not the best idea! Develop, but do not lose focus!

#10·1 To read

We tried to give some book recommendations embedded in the previous chapters, but there are still countless useful books waiting to be read. This is a randomly picked collection of books we like(d) and suggest. Here you can find leadership, business, behavioral economics and self development books as well. Remember: leaders are leaders.

Monetizing innovation
by Madhavan Ramanujam and Georg Tacke

The art of war
by Sun Tzu

Ego is the enemy
By Ryan Holiday

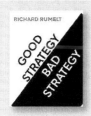

Good strategy, bad strategy
by Richard Rumelt

Embracing your inner critic
by Hal Stone and Sidra Stone

No rules rules
by Reed Hastings, Erin Meyer, et al.

Effective executive
by Peter F. Drucker

The lean startup
by Eric Ries

Your five next moves
by Patrick Bet-David

Radical candor
by Kim Scott

Disciplined entrepreneurship
by Bill Aulet

Inspired
by Marty Cagan

Noise
by Daniel Kahneman, Olivier Sibony, et al.

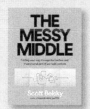

The messy middle
by Scott Belsky

Effortless experience
by Matthew Dixon, Nick Toman, et al.

Leadership is language
by L. David Marquet and Penguin Audio

The startup owner's manual
by Steve Blank and Bob Dorf

The four steps to the epiphany
by Steve Blank

Good to great
by Jim Collins

Built to last
by Jim Collins

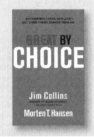

Great by choice
by Jim Collins

Scaling up
by Verne Harnish

How I built this
by Guy Raz

Zero to one
by Peter Thiel, Blake Masters, et al.

Crossing the chasm
by Geoffrey A. Moore

Hooked
by Nir Eyal and Ryan Hoover

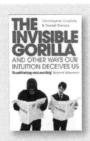

The invisible gorilla
by Christopher Chabris and Daniel Simons

Predictably irrational
by Dr. Dan Ariely

The five dysfunctions of a team
by Patrick Lencioni

Quiet Leadership
by David Rock

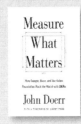

Measure what matters
by John Doerr and Larry Page

The effective manager
by Mark Horstman

The infinite game
by Simon Sinek

Start with why
by Simon Sinek

Principles
by Ray Dalio

The Culture code
by Daniel Coyle, Will Damron, et al.

#10·2 To watch/listen

There is more and more useful content on Youtube, Twitch, Tik-Tok and many other platforms. Some big incubators, accelerators and other ecosystem members are regularly uploading videos worth watching and more and more big universities share parts of their teaching materials with the wider public. These entities have tons of knowledge, are experienced and know the tips and tricks you would probably learn only in ten years time, so they are worth your time! Sometimes you need to pay for these resources, but – especially with the pandemic – more and more parties have shared smaller pieces of information without any fees. Free knowledge everywhere!

I am an auditory learner, so I mostly consume audiobooks and podcasts instead of reading the books themselves. Many items of our lists above are also available in an audible format. It is your choice how you would like to consume it!

If you have a limited amount of time, you can even connect 'lost time' and consuming this media while doing sports in the gym, or during a nice walk outside.

#10·3 To follow

It is always a good idea to follow big thinkers, influencers, specialists, opinion leaders, and proven doers. It is almost like having a good mentor. Not as personalized, but you can get a lot of information just by consuming their content and learning from them. You do not have to reinvent everything by yourself!

#11 About us

This book is a collaboration of two initiatives, disRaptors and Ability Matrix, written by András Bence-Kiss, featured by Ákos Tolnai as contributor and professional mentor. By this, both the business knowledge (product-market fit) and the industry experience are merged and represented in one single piece.

András Bence-Kiss,
the tribe leader of disRaptors

Personally, I am an engineer – a material engineer to be exact – but I have also studied mechanical engineering. Besides that, I am a generalist, a fallen startupper, a start-up mentor, who has worked for and with startups meanwhile working in classical companies as a quality engineer (both on supplier and customer side), and project management team leader.

Working on the edge of these two worlds made me realize that I can be the bridge between them since I understand the needs of startups and the way they see the world, while also being familiar with the industry, production companies, quality assurance, and several technologies. I love seeing startups and conservative manufacturing companies grow together and my soul cries when they cannot align.

I tried to develop competencies that make me valuable support for both parties. Throughout my career, I have realized that I am good at collecting information and turning it into patterns by understanding the dynamics. My brain just refuses everything without a logical pattern or insight, which does not bring me further on my journey. This helps me bridge the gaps of understanding, culture, and communication between the different parties.

My experience of the last decade, seeing startups making the same mistakes, and the urge to drive change brought me to the idea to write this book and make disRaptors happen.

About disRaptors

We chose the name with my cofounder, Daniel, because we are fascinated by everything from dinosaurs to the latest tech developments and we are seeking innovation and disruption everywhere. We would like to understand the world, understand ourselves and find the way we can support people like you, how to do the same.

Shortly before I started writing, we sat together with Daniel, who is one of my best friends, and tried to find the solution to the world's biggest problems as usual. That was when we came to the conclusion that we needed to build something we wished to have been there for some years ago.

I consider Daniel as a genius needing to learn to focus his energy and to channel it into innovation. His superpower is having a strategic eye combined with a knowledge-hungry brain. We both are open-minded, curious generalists, who cannot sit still in a small city in the middle of the CEE region without building something meaningful. We are bridge- and world-builders with BHAGs not everybody understands.

There are many people like us, who are struggling; forcing themselves into roles they do not fit, where they cannot give the world the value they could. Our view is that we need to make the opportunities for ourselves and not wait for them. They will not come without effort for sure.

This is why disRaptors was born. To collect and support thinkers, doers, innovators, disruptors, and other high-potential individuals, who cannot find their place in the world, just because the location and timing are not right, or good mentors are out of their reach.

disRaptors is meant to give hope and support to innovators of many kinds. We have a 30-year-plan ahead. As the first step – by this book – we help great products get produced, and parallel we build a bridge to other innovators by merging the gaming and esports strategies with the startup and entrepreneurship best practices.

The HW startup related part of the disRaptors masterplan looks like

1. Writing this book
2. Helping HW startups in project management and roadmap planning
3. Giving HW startups specialized project managers.
4. Teaching Hardware startups to project management and roadmap planning
5. Helping HW startups reach production SOP (start of production
6. Supporting HW startups with engineering capacity, prototyping, and engineering builds
7. Providing a place for the first engineering builds, also engineering, and project management support
8. HW startup accelerator with engineers for development and production, necessary equipment, and place. Startups can join programs with accommodation at our place.
9. Turning disRaptors into something even bigger.

Join us, help us or let us help you!

You can find us at disraptors.tech or write an email to me directly at andras@disraptors.tech.

Krisztina Bence-Kiss

 I am the odd one out here, since I am not and have never been an engineer myself. I am an economist, more precisely a marketing specialist specialized in online- and social media marketing; and also an associate professor of this field, which seems to be pretty far from the HW startup environment.

However, being the wife of a startupper in itself has already provided me with a certain level of insight into the topic: I have seen the ups, downs and the traps of entering such a volatile environment as a newcomer. I have always been interested in the startup environment, which has also been one of my research areas, but being too much of a risk averse person I have never actually engaged in any startup activities.

Owning a small business myself too, I have experience in team-management and business issues – though not related to hardware at all –, which made me an 'outsider-insider' in this book.

Ákos Tolnai, Founder, AbilityMatrix

 I started AbilityMatrix with the intention to help innovators become more successful. I believe that our knowledge can speed up innovation cycles and go-to-market and it is our duty to help innovators avoid failure and keep them "sane" through the valley of death.

I have mostly been an early adopter of almost any new technology. I have already had smartphones when you still had to charge them several times a day and needed to hack the registry to make it work.

After a short stint as a software developer and later another as the head of software development, I quickly switched to different sales positions in IT. Working as a key account or leading teams as a regional manager, my focus was mostly on developing the skills of my team and myself. Constantly reinventing ourselves and trying to keep the edge were my mantras.

The journey of building AbilityMatrix has been the journey of my life. Amazing stories that could fill a book highlighted my path to validating the method and eventually finding what the market would buy from us as a service. Ups and downs, a lot of amazing people helping at the different stages of my journey, and now, as we are a team of 15+ people, helping you, the AbilityMatrix Team.

I believe that success is temporary and sometimes out of your control. The things you learn and people you meet are the most important takeaways that will help and serve you through the rest of your life as an innovator, as a family man, or as a volunteer. My goal is to have a positive impact on as many people as humanly possible, especially in the innovation and customer experience community. Making innovators more successful will eventually help save the Earth and "outinnovate" our extinction.

I try to close the loop by paying forward and helping startups in the early stages just like other people have helped me – and still keep helping me. The camaraderie and support that are present in the innovation community are the fuel that keeps me going.

About AbilityMatrix

AbilityMatrix is a consulting company helping innovators succeed. Built around an in-house behavior-based segmentation model, we have developed several frameworks supporting the early phase of startups and corporate innovations alike.

The company focuses on providing three critical elements of the early-stage startup life needed for survival:

Insights to understand customers, market dynamics, and go-to-market strategy better.

Knowledge to adapt, execute and strategize the further steps and eventually continue without the support of AbilityMatrix.

Leads to prove the experiments. Customers paying for services are the final and unquestionable proof of any assumption.

The two frameworks we created in the company help in go-to-market and product-market fit, both by using applied behavioral science in the B2B segment.

The Go-To-Market Matrix uses behavioral problem-decision maker matching to create a structured approach to testing for a better and faster understanding of B2B markets. This supports faster pivots and better insights from fewer data.

The Product-Market Fit matrix helps product teams and C-level executives understand better what drives perceived value to customers. It helps prioritize the product backlog and balance the workload. By better understanding customer irrationalities, they can improve price elasticity. The product-market fit matrix combines features, insights, and strategic assets into one comprehensive view.

The company works with startups, digital SMBs, and corporate innovation labs. With offices in Toronto, (ON, Canada) Vienna, (Austria) Budapest, (Hungary) we bring the best from the European and North American ecosystem to our clients since 2011.

You can reach the AbilityMatrix team on our webpage, abilitymatrix.com, by booking a call, or directly by my direct mail: tolnai@abilitymatrix.com.

#12 Acknowledgement

Hi,
this is András here.

Writing a book is harder than I thought and more rewarding than I could have ever imagined. None of this would have been possible without my wife. Kriszti was there not just as a wife, but also as emotional support, proofreader, and general support team to reduce the load on me in all other fields of life. She did so much for this book to happen, that she evolved to be a coauthor. She stood by me during all the struggles and all my successes. That is true love, and also friendship.

Besides my wife, my friend and featuring author, Ákos Tolnai was the person who made this possible. His insights, mentoring, and the parts of the book he wrote completed my knowledge and competence. He is also a role model for me with AbilityMatrix, the company he has built and leads since then. He has the mindset of an innovative CEO, which is rare in this region and keeps inspiring me with his good questions at the right moment. The structure of this book could not be as good as it is now, had he not been challenging me. Thank you Ákos!

I could not be more thankful to my family. My parents supported me, especially throughout my studies and development beyond their possibilities.

Having an idea and turning it into a book is as hard as it sounds. The experience is both internally challenging and rewarding. I especially want to thank the individuals, who helped me make this happen. On the technical side, I would like to thank Bence Borsos, founder of Booxpert, who guided me through the journey. It was a common adventure since Publishdrive was also new to him.

Pre- and proofreaders were important and essential companions on the journey.

I am also thankful to people, companies, and institutions who taught and supported me as a friend, partner, employer, mentor, coach, friend, or mentoree. Without claiming completeness:

- The people I currently work together with, cooperating through the ups and downs of our projects and the daily challenges we face together
  - Máté Horváth, my direct manager, who has always supported my weird ideas on how the company should work. His perseverance is almost heroic.
  - Balázs Fináncz, who is an example of an internal hero.
  - István Lak, the humble and wise friend, whom I could always call.
  - Tamás Megyeri, who knows the best how challenging it can be with startups as a traditional CM.
  - The project management team I am honored to lead. These guys taught me lessons not just in project management, but also in being a good human.

  The experience I gained here taught me a lot. The insights I had here are priceless and served as a valuable resource to this book. Gratitude for Videoton grows together with the experience I gain there.

- I am grateful to Bosch (RBHH and RBHU), Electrolux Kft. Floorcare division, Som-Plast Kft, the companies I have also worked for, and all the colleagues, who took part in my professional training, shaping my knowledge and sharpening my eyes, with special thanks to the Quality department of Electrolux and Károly Béda.
- Input Program (with PwC), and CEU iLabs mentor programs. It was a big step forward to take part in both of these programs and meet and learn from all these wonderful people:
  - Balázs Gyenese – the person responsible for the Input Mentor Program – gave me more than just conducting the sessions. He became a friend, a mentor, and a coach in my life. His dedication to raising other people gives all of us a very positive message.
  - Márton Kovács, the local face of the Input program, pushed me to become a mentor. I cannot be thankful enough for that, Marci!
  - In the programs, I met great people, who transformed my knowledge. They give me the power and endurance to keep going forward.
- I am thankful to Qatalyst, my first startup. This journey was more than a lesson, it was THE LESSON, the rollercoaster of my life. Great ups, less great downs. Without this I would be less resilient, and less...everything. It could not have happened without
  - László Ákos Pál, my co-founder and all the colleagues we worked together with. I am sorry for the bad decisions I made. It had to be this way.
  - Hiventures, Hungarian venture capital fund for the trust and investment.

- ◦ Csaba Schuck, friend and master of business models, financial models, and the execution of a financial plan.
  - ◦ Balázs Tornai, Bala, and his team for the professional support reinventing Qatalyst and turning it into code.
- instagrid GmbH, one of the hottest battery startups in the EU. Great founders, great team, great project. It was a challenging journey, but what you did and are still doing is amazing. Please never stop!
- Refilamer, the startup turning PET bottles into 3D printing filament. I am thankful for the time spent with you and I am ready to support you in the future as well.
  I am especially thankful for Hunor Kiri, the founder of Refilamer, whose development is the rise of a true CEO. Keep up the good work, Hunor!
- And of course all the HW startups I have met and worked with

I would also like to mention the disRaptor support team I am thankful to and proud to work with. Dániel Stirling, my friend, and cofounder, Dániel Dobos helped with the website, and Bence Ragány, who turned my vision into a brand design. We still have a lot to do, guys!

Last but not least, big thanks to the nameless heroes on the internet, who shared their content as free to use, without any legal restrictions, e.g. the Unsplash community and their wonderful photos I could use.